Simone Weil
Waiting on Truth

Berg Women's Series

Gertrude Bell — Susan Goodman
Mme de Staël — Renee Winegarten
Emily Dickinson — Donna Dickenson
Elizabeth Gaskell — Tessa Brodetsky
Mme du Châtelet — Esther Ehrmann
Emily Carr — Ruth Gowers
George Sand — Donna Dickenson
Simone de Beauvoir — Renee Winegarten
Sigrid Undset — Mitzi Brundsdale
Willa Cather — Jamie Ambrose
Elizabeth I — Susan Bassnett
Margaret Fuller — David Watson

In preparation

Mme de Sevigné — Jeanne A. and William T. Ojala
Anna Freud — Renee Paton
Dorothy Sayers — Mitzi Brunsdale
Rosa Luxemburg — Richard Abraham
Mary Wollstonecraft — Jennifer Lorch

Simone Weil

Waiting on Truth

J.P. Little

BERG *Oxford/New York/Hamburg*
Distributed exclusively in the US and Canada by
St Martin's Press, New York

First published in 1988 by
Berg Publishers Limited
77 Morrell Avenue, Oxford, OX4 1NQ, UK
175 Fifth Avenue/Room 400, New York, NY 10010, USA
Nordalbingerweg 14, 2000 Hamburg 61, FRG

© J.P. Little 1988

All rights reserved.
No part of this publication may be reproduced
in any form or by any means without the written permission
of Berg Publishers Limited

British Library Cataloguing in Publication Data
Little, J.P. (Janet Patricia), *1941–*
  Simone Weil, J.P. Little. (Berg women's
  series).
  1. French philosophy. Weil, Simone, 1909–
  1943. Biographies
  I. Title
  194

ISBN 0–85496–165–8

Library of Congress Cataloging-in-Publication Data
Little, J.P.
  Simone Weil / J.P. Little.
     p. cm. — (Berg women's series)
  Bibliography: p.
  Includes index.
  ISBN 0–85496–165–8: $35.00 (U.S.: est.)
  1. Weil, Simone, 1909–1943. I. Title. II. Series.
B2430.W474L57 1988
194—dc19
[B]   87–37397
                                                                          CIP

Printed in Great Britain by Billing & Sons Ltd, Worcester

Contents

Introduction	1
Part I A Life in its Context	5
Part II The Works	51
1 The Good and the Necessary	53
2 The Great Beast	67
3 The Need for Roots	84
4 The Theory and Practice of Work	105
5 The *Via Negativa*	120
6 Mediators and Mediation	135
Towards a Conclusion	151
Chronology	157
Select Bibliography	161
Index	167

Illustrations

Between pages 86 and 87
1. Simone with her father, Dr Bernard Weil, Mayenne (1915–1916)
2. Mme Selma Weil, Simone's mother
3. Simone with her brother André, Knokke-le-Zoute (1922)
4. Spain (1936)
5. Marseille (Spring 1941)
6. Simone Weil in New York (1942)
7. Manuscript copy by Simone Weil of George Herbert's poem 'Love'
8. Extract from the 'Factory Journal'
9. Simone's conclusions on her factory experience
10. Cover of one of Simone's Notebooks
11. Page from one of the Notebooks (1941)
12. Page from one of the Notebooks (1942)
13. Beginning of a draft for the 'Declaration of obligations . . .' (London 1943)

Photos 1, 3, 4, 5, 6, courtesy Mlle Simone Pétrement
Photo 2 courtesy Mrs Elsie Fischer
Photos 7–13 (manuscripts) courtesy Prof. André Weil

Abbreviations

Abbreviations used in the text (for full reference, see Bibliography)

AD	*Attente de Dieu*
C1	*Cahiers*, I
C2	*Cahiers*, II
C3	*Cahiers*, III
CO	*La Condition ouvrière*
CS	*La Connaissance surnaturelle*
EH	*Ecrits historiques et politiques*
EL	*Ecrits de Londres et dernières lettres*
E	*L'Enracinement*
IP	*Intuitions pré-chrétiennes*
LR	*Lettre à un religieux*
OL	*Oppression et liberté*
PSO	*Pensées sans ordre concernant l'amour de Dieu*
P	*Poèmes, suivis de 'Venise sauvée'*
SG	*La Source grecque*
SS	*Sur la science*

These abbreviations are followed immediately by the page reference, in the style *EH* 49.

Reference is to the French edition of these texts, but quotations appear in the author's translation. For quotations of fifteen words and more, the original French is given in the Notes at the end of each chapter.

Acknowledgements

This study is the fruit of a long-standing fascination with the work of Simone Weil, and it is impossible to thank all the many people who have contributed to my understanding of its richness and complexity. My early conversations with Louis Allen, of the University of Durham, opened my eyes to many of the issues raised by Simone Weil, and over the years contact with the members of the *Association pour l'étude de la pensée de Simone Weil* has deepened my understanding of these issues. The Camargo Foundation, Cassis, generously afforded me the material conditions and the necessary break from the everyday which allowed me to give my undivided attention to the project. To all I express my sincere gratitude, as to my husband, whose patience and clear-sighted criticism has followed and sustained my itinary throughout.

J.P.L.

Dun Laoghaire

Introduction

Any attempt to recount the life of Simone Weil brings us immediately up against a contradiction: how can we talk about the life of someone who spent her whole time trying to reduce the sense of the personal and the anecdotal? Up to the very end she insisted that what mattered was not herself as an individual, but what she had to say. Her message was in a sense totally independent of its medium, and she always claimed not only that it was not personal to her, but that she did not understand how or why it had chosen such an inadequate and defective vehicle as herself for its transmission.

A related problem is the very nature of that life. It is only too easy to emphasise the picturesque and the dramatic in an existence as extraordinary as that of Simone Weil. The temptation to hagiography too is great, and those who have succumbed to it have frequently been inspired in all good faith by the accounts of those who knew her and worked with her. She was clearly not the sort of person to go unnoticed in any context. Sometimes this feature has been used to underline the bizarre, almost the grotesque, in the personality, so that one is left wondering how so alarmingly abnormal a character could possibly have written what she did. Just as she aroused strong reaction during her life, so her writings have continued to provoke controversy. Belonging to no one, no group or faction, pointing to what she saw to be the truth in and out of season, she has often managed to alienate both Right and Left, each side recognising certain features of her thought, but in the end unable to appropriate her.

The unity of her life and thought implied here creates a further problem of presentation. Her writings are at times almost incomprehensible without a knowledge of the life that produced them, just as some of the episodes of her life can be understood adequately only in the context of her thought. Simone Weil herself, in a review of a book on Karl Marx, warns against recounting the life of great men without reference to their work.[1] To do so, she says, results in highlighting their petty features, since they have put the best of themselves into their work. Worse still, their everyday vanities are often presented as the price to be paid for genius, so that the reader is obliged to conclude that genius always resides in an intolerable human being, while superior moral qualities are the prerogative of the mediocre. She maintains that a way of solving this problem is to look for signs of greatness in the lives of the great, greatness which is fully manifest only in their work, not hiding their human failings, but interpreting them as the limit and not the essence of genius. I shall have cause to bear in mind her warning in the following pages and, while giving a biographical sketch in the first part, will return to and develop in a more extended second part many of the points made here.

Another fact to be borne in mind is just how brief Simone Weil's life was. When reviewing the extent of her writings — the projected 'Complete Works' in the original French will run to some sixteen volumes[2] — and considering the historical events she participated in, it is hard to realise that she was only thirty-four when she died. This means that she had had no time for retrospection, no time to become 'a classic' in her own lifetime, no mature years to enjoy the recognition which her writings would undoubtedly have brought her, and no opportunity of explaining herself to her public even if she had wanted to. (One wonders what Simone Weil would have made of the media in the 1980s.) All her writings are fragmentary, many circumstantial, and she did not write one single book-length piece for publication. Much of her writing is, indeed, in the form of notebooks, where she disciplined herself to jot down, day by day, ideas that came to her, some of which were subsequently used in essays and articles for publication, some not. There is no doubt that, although some of her writing is astonishingly mature, she was nevertheless still evolving on every level. The pace of that evolution was partly governed by the period of European history through which she lived. Her mature years coincided with the social upheavals occasioned by the economic depression of the 1930s, the rise of Hitler and Nazi Gemany, the Spanish Civil War, and the first four years of the Second World War. All these events were agonising for someone as socially aware as Simone Weil and, like other Europeans of her time, she was constantly and brutally brought face to face with impossible choices, impossible in the sense that the best to be hoped for was to discern the lesser evil and opt for that.

In these circumstances, any presentation of what Simone Weil did or wrote must necessarily be tentative. In particular, any overview of her writings suffers from the fact that no single critic can be expert in all the fields that her wide-ranging and passionate curiosity and formidable intellectual energy touched upon and frequently assimilated. In terms of the general context, one has the good fortune of referring to a recent period in European history, and one that is well-documented (while remaining subject still to the passions of those who lived through it), while her biography has already been well-researched, notably by her friend and fellow-philosopher, Simone Pétrement, to whose excellent biographical study[3] my debt will be obvious in the following pages, but also, at an earlier period, by critics such as Jacques Cabaud.[4] My purpose throughout is to provoke a return to the texts themselves: in Simone Weil's lucid prose can be found all that she was concerned to say, and which she said with ever-increasing urgency, mindful of the 'deposit of pure gold' which she had to transmit, and more and more desperate at finding so few ready to receive it.

Notes

1. 'Otto Rühle: *Karl Marx*', *La Critique Sociale*, II, Mar. 34, pp. 246–7.
2. The first volume is now available: Simone Weil, *Oeuvres Complètes*, new edn, vol. I, *Premiers Essais Philosophiques*, Paris: Gallimard, 1988.
3. Simone Pétrement, *La Vie de Simone Weil*, 2 vols., Paris: Fayard, 1973.
4. See notably his *Simone Weil: A Fellowship in Love* London: Harvill, 1964; New York: Channel Press, 1965, and *Simone Weil à New York et à Londres: Les quinze derniers mois (1942–3)*, Paris: Plon, 1967.

Part I A Life in its Context

Simone Weil was born in Paris on 3 February 1909 into a bourgeois Jewish family, her father of Alsatian origin, her mother Austrian. Her father, a doctor, was inevitably often absent from the home. Madame Weil, on the other hand, was free to devote her considerable energy and intelligence to the upbringing of her two children, Simone and her brother André, three years her senior. At birth Simone thrived, but from six months to around her second birthday suffered a whole series of health problems, and at one point was not expected to survive. Although she recovered after that and began to develop normally, this setback almost certainly had a bearing on her future poor health.

Her early childhood was a happy one, however. It was a lively, cultured family, held together by a strong bond of affection which manifested itself frequently in ironic wit and repartee. Both children showed signs of precocious intelligence, especially André, who later became a renowned mathematician and who, according to Simone, had a childhood similar to Pascal's. They spent much of their early childhood together, playing games which were frequently intellectual in nature. They would make up verse impromptu, or learn long passages from the French classical writers, which they would then act. In spite of Simone's very obvious affection for her brother, which continued into adulthood, she seems to have developed an inferiority complex towards him. His gifts indeed were so extraordinary and so precocious that it is perhaps understandable that she began to underestimate her own very considerable intellect.

Simone was only five when the First World War broke out, and thereafter for four years the family lived a very disrupted existence, following Doctor Weil on his various postings in France. The two children were very conscious of the war that was going on around them: they gave up their sugar-ration for the soldiers at the Front, and corresponded with their 'filleuls de guerre', soldiers who were 'adopted' by families for the duration of the war, and to whom the children sent parcels of food and small treats, put together with money they had collected. One of

Simone's earliest genuinely political reactions occurred at the Armistice, where the deliberate humiliation of Germany shocked and angered her. During this period the children's school attendance was spasmodic: Simone was still delicate, and although she began to attend the Lycée Montaigne in Paris and then the *lycée* at Laval, there were long periods when she had a private tutor at home, when it seems she enjoyed a good deal of latitude in what she did. Although the war situation was clearly exceptional, it seems that this attitude to education fitted in well with Madame Weil's ideas on the subject. Schools and private tutors were always chosen with a view to developing creative excellence in the children; Madame Weil went instinctively to the top, so that when Simone began piano lessons, for instance, although she showed no talent for the instrument, Germaine Tailleferre was engaged as teacher. Madame Weil was also convinced that some things were worth doing and others not, and Simone was allowed gradually to drop subjects that she found too difficult. Map-work in geography, and drawing, eventually disappeared from her timetable, because she had, and always would have, great problems of manipulation. Nothing was left to chance, therefore, and from the start, with Madame Weil's encouragement, Simone was allowed to develop her natural love of literature, and later philosophy, while participating to the best of her ability in her brother's development in mathematics.

His abilities were such that, as I have suggested, the situation seems to have provoked a crisis in Simone during her adolescence. In a letter written to the priest Father Perrin towards the end of her life[1] she tells how the extraordinary abilities of her brother had convinced her of the 'mediocrity' of her natural gifts, and of her despair at thus being denied access to the realm of truth reserved for genius. After months of hopelessness, however, she suddenly had the conviction that anyone, no matter how limited his natural faculties, could have access to this realm, provided that he desires truth and makes a constant effort of attention to attain it. This moment of realisation was of immense importance: not only did it release her from her deep adolescent depression, but it provided inspiration in all her subsequent development, both for herself and in her efforts in the education of others. Many a time she would take it upon herself to coach children or adults she came across in mathematics or philosophy, even when, or especially when, her pupils seemed very modestly endowed with natural talent. Talent, for Simone Weil, was irrelevant, and could even be a handicap in the development of genius. Genius involved going beyond the natural faculties to a different order of perception; to boast of high intellectual endowment was like being in prison and boasting of having a larger cell than the other prisoners.

It is probably during adolescence, too, that she began to reject her own femininity, seeing in it perhaps something which could deflect her from her pursuit of truth. It seems she was very pretty as a child, and friends and callers at the house would praise the Weils for their children, 'genius and beauty'. So thoughtless although well-meant a remark, opposing apparently exclusively the intellectual and the physical, could not have failed to make an impression on a child as sensitive as Simone.

During the whole of this childhood period Simone had received no religious instruction from any source. Her parents were not practising Jews, although it seems that her paternal grandparents, in particular her grandmother, were. Their Jewish origins must have been one of the few subjects not freely discussed in the Weil household, since it appears that Simone was ten before she learned she was Jewish, and that there was a difference between Jew and Gentile. Maybe, totally assimilated as they were, the question simply seemed irrelevant. Christianity was always the religion with which she was most familiar: she was later to declare that her whole life had been imbued with manifestations of Christian culture, with which she had always felt perfectly at home.

In 1925, when she was sixteen, Simone entered the Lycée Henri-IV in Paris where she was enrolled in the *Première supérieure*, the preparation class for the Ecole Normale Supérieure, one of the *Grandes Ecoles*, and therefore one of the pinnacles of achievement in the highly intellectual and competitive French educational system. There she had a decisive meeting with Alain, pseudonym of Emile Chartier, the philosopher whose teaching had a profound influence on a whole generation of French youth, and who was her teacher at Henri-IV for three years, although in fact, so deep was her attachment that she and other students continued to return to his classes when they had left the *lycée*. He was a radical who taught his students to be wary of 'les pouvoirs', the powers-that-be, authority in all its forms, the State, the Church — in short, the collective that corrupts all. He also taught, however, a concern for order which in his view was just as important. 'Resistance and obedience, those are the two virtues of the citizen', he would say, the virtue of obedience being necessary to ensure order. His was a philosophy of 'la volonté', the will, in so far as virtue for him was a question of governing one's passions; one's first duty is to oneself, and if one accomplishes that correctly, one cannot fail to do one's duty to others at the same time. This notion of responsibility for one's own life deeply influenced Simone, as did his moral philosophy in general. While Alain made a great impact on her, however, he, in turn, was clearly greatly impressed by her. In the end-of-term reports he wrote on her, he notes her exceptional gifts, predicting a brilliant future for her, and warning her only to be on her guard against too great a degree of abstraction and subtlety in her reasoning.

During her time at Henri-IV, Simone, in common with many of her classmates, put into practice Alain's ideas on challenging authority, and it is here that she gained her reputation for rebelliousness which was to stay with her throughout her early career. Alain's students rapidly developed a consciousness of two standards, whether in academic work or behaviour, the 'normal' one, which got you through examinations and ensured that you stayed on the right side of authority, and the one Alain taught. Simone acquired a reputation for being a Communist, but it is certain that she never joined the Party. Although, according to Boris Souvarine, she was attracted to it at one point, she rejected the idea of joining in the end because friends she esteemed had suffered exclusion on the orders of Moscow. She was certainly conscious very early on of the deficiencies of Communism as practised, and naturally suspicious of its inherent collectivism. Temperamentally, she inclined towards small, informal groups. But with her youthful taste for provocation, she did nothing to discourage the rumours that went round concerning her. Any involvement with left-wing causes or with the less fortunate in society would have been enough to start these going. It was certainly natural that at this stage she should react against what she must have seen as her highly privileged background. One must remember the hierarchical nature of French society during this period, and the extent to which privilege still operated. Free secondary schooling was not, after all, established until 1933, and the universities and the higher echelons of the *lycées* were very much a bourgeois prerogative. Students could not fail to see themselves as a privileged section of society, and the more sensitive of them to react against this situation in one way or another. In Simone's case this took the form of much political discussion of a theoretical nature, but also an immediate involvement in projects for the under-privileged, the most notable being the *Groupe d'éducation sociale*, a sort of Workers' Educational Organisation, set up by the students, who gave courses in language, mathematics and physics, as well as 'social education', dealing with political and social matters. The idea was to equip working people with the language and intellectual skills needed to assume power over their own destiny, as well as giving them the basis of a genuine culture. It is characteristic that even at this stage Simone Weil did not see the righting of social evils purely, or even essentially, in economic terms. While a certain basic financial security was necessary to well-being, at least as important were the things of the mind, so that working people could liberate themselves from the slavery induced by their lack of understanding of the industrial and other processes to which they were subjected. Simone was an early participant in this scheme, therefore, where she taught mainly political subjects. She passed the section of the course on feminism over to a colleague, however, declaring that she was not a feminist.

This assertion is perfectly consistent with her attitude to her own femininity, which we have already touched on. Throughout her career she demonstrated a refusal to side with groups with which she might have been thought to have an identity of interest. Her refusal to single out Jewish victims of persecution before and during the war, when she was constantly giving help to refugees of all kinds, is probably a reflection of the same tendency; certainly one of the reasons for her hostility to the Jewish cause was their desire, as she saw it, to set themselves apart from the rest of humanity. She saw her role as identifying with the wretched of the earth without distinction, and militated precisely for those groups with whom she could not be said to have anything in common save their humanity. Ironically, had she been born into the working class, she might well have found it more difficult to identify with working people, and to militate on their behalf.

If she seems during her student years to have increasingly refused her femininity, this refusal probably has a range of origins. First of all, she must have been conscious that for someone with the desire to accomplish what she wanted to, being born a woman was a very definite handicap. In France at this time women had no political rights; they were enfranchised only in 1944, had no right to property, required the permission of their husband to run a business, or obtain a passport. Many professions were closed to them, including diplomacy, the magistrature and the more important branches of medicine. In the world of education, women were only just beginning to be taken seriously: they had been admitted to the Lycée Henri-IV only a year before Simone entered, and at the Ecole Normale she found herself in an all-male class. While an elite were beginning to get the opportunity for prolonged education, it was still a man's world, and competition was on male terms. To achieve distinction in the world of learning it was neither relevant nor advantageous to be a woman, and Simone was not the first — or the last — to draw the obvious conclusions. Her refusal to dress in an acceptably feminine manner, and adopt feminine graces, can also be read as a parallel to her refusal to please through personal seduction, which is clear in every aspect of her life. She saw the art of pleasing, when it takes priority over the pursuit of truth, as somehow dishonest, and she was too pure and too utterly honest a character to want to play games with people, either on the intellectual or the emotional level. Much better in fact to put people off, even to repel them, and then if in spite of this they offered friendship, you knew you were making contact on the level of truth. In any case, one wonders whether the question of the ultimate rejection of an intimate part of herself would have arisen if Simone Weil had been a man. The desire to please is not normally taken into consideration when assessing male genius, after all.

The lack of attention to her appearance was also due of course to the fact that she was intensely and passionately committed to her studies and other preoccupations, and this is how she herself explained it. Her intellectual interests, under Alain's influence, were almost exclusively in philosophy at this time, so much so that she failed the examination for the Ecole Normale the first time she presented herself, due mainly to a lack of attention to history. By the time she did pass it, the following year in 1928, she had also passed the four certificates necessary for the philosophy degree from the Sorbonne.

At the Ecole Normale she remained loyal to Alain, both by continuing to attend his classes unofficially at Henri-IV, and by her rejection of most of the teachers who had the misfortune to come after him. Even very eminent scholars such as Henri Brunschvicg were given a testing time by previous pupils of Alain, lacking his magnetism and going against many of the ideas that his pupils held sacred. The Assistant Director of the Ecole Normale, Bouglé, had a particularly rough ride with Simone: Jacques Cabaud in his biography tells the story of one of her challenges to his authority when, at a loss for an adequate reply, he took out his watch and said: 'It's mid-day. Let's go and have lunch'. This naturally became a catch-phrase, repeated with great glee and the appropriate accompanying gesture whenever anyone could not find the answer to a question.

During her time at the Ecole Normale Simone developed many of the other tendencies that had begun to be manifest already at the *lycée*. She began to move in pacifist circles, and took part in a pacifist petition organised by the students. What the students were demanding in fact was the right not to undergo military training which led to their being automatically drafted as officers. They wished to do military service as simple conscripts, thereby refusing the seal of approval to the Army and the military establishment in general. The petition caused a great scandal, not only at the Ecole Normale but in the national press, given the attitude which such demands implied.

Simone also continued work at the *Groupe d'éducation sociale* in the rue Falguière, this time teaching mainly French. She was increasingly interested in both the theory and practice of work, and two of her early articles, written for Alain's journal *Libres Propos*, are precisely on this subject. She became more and more anxious to experience the reality of physical labour — again, probably a reaction against her background — and in the summer of 1929 worked for a spell on the land in the Jura. While still at Henri-IV she had spent time helping on a friend's farm, and it is clear from her account of it that the experience gave her a very special joy. From then until her death agricultural labour was to be for her a privileged way of entering into contact with the reality of the universe, a privilege which she exercised whenever she could, and she took a naïve pleasure in keeping up with other, more seasoned workers.

During these years she also joined the first women's rugby club, a fact which is noteworthy mainly because of the superhuman determination with which she threw herself into the game. Undeterred by injury or fatigue, she was the admiration of all those who saw her. Admiration and respect were common among the attitudes adopted towards her by her fellow-students. There was also a certain amount of mockery, not always well-meant, maybe the reverse side of the awkwardness some of them felt in her presence. She had a way of 'confronting you with your responsibilities', which was discomfiting to those who could not live with the world's sufferings permanently on their shoulders. She had begun to be concerned by the situation of France's overseas possessions, a concern, she later recounts, which was sparked off by the articles written by Louis Roubaud in *Le Petit Parisien* at the time of the Colonial Exhibition in Paris in 1931.[2] These articles told of the suffering and oppression experienced by the Annamites in what is now North and South Vietnam and this was what made her understand for the first time the tragedy of colonisation. She was to remain enormously sensitive to France's behaviour in its colonial territories, experiencing a deep sense of shame at any manifestation of injustice.

Although her left-wing tendencies gave her a reputation for Marxist if not out-and-out Communist sympathies, there is evidence that she was not entirely closed to religious ideas, either at this point or at other moments in her childhood and youth. At the Ecole Normale she was known occasionally to support a religious point of view, even in the course of one conversation suggesting that she might become a nun. Also, at around the same time, she declared that she could not understand people who did not believe in God. Even earlier, at the Lycée Victor Duruy, she was greatly impressed by the young Edi Copeau, daughter of the theatrical director Jacques Copeau, who was already showing signs of a religious vocation. When later she entered the Benedictine order, Simone apparently showed towards her an 'ardent, almost tender approval'. It is important to retain these indications of a sympathy for a religious view of life, in order to avoid the narrowing division of Simone Weil's life into a militant, agnostic, period, followed by a mystical 'conversion'.

Her academic activities at the Ecole Normale were centered on intensive preparation for the highly competitive teaching examination, the *Agrégation*, and on her *Diplôme d'Etudes Supérieures*, which had the philosophy of Descartes as its subject. This diploma, which is a serious but free-ranging development of Descartes's philosophy in the Sorbonne manner, rather than a work of detailed research, was disapproved of by Brunschvicg who assessed it, giving her a bare pass mark. In the *Agrégation* she passed, but not as well as might have been expected: she came only seventh. Nevertheless it seems to have been the months of intensive intellectual effort leading up to the *Agrégation* that set off the first of the crippling headaches from which she was to suffer for the rest of her life. Their cause was never properly diagnosed, although a form of sinusitis was eventually suggested. A number of different treatments were tried, but nothing brought more than temporary relief, although the headaches were perhaps less severe from 1939 onwards. She occasionally describes in letters to friends the devastating effect they had on her: she seriously considered suicide more than once, and they were almost entirely responsible for the prolonged sick-leave which she had to take from her teaching on several occasions. They clearly had a radical effect on her view of reality, as well as on her relationships with others.

With the *Agrégation* behind her, Simone was a fully-qualified philosophy teacher and ready to take up a post. She asked to be sent to an industrial town so that she could develop her interest in the industrial process: she had in fact been undecided as to whether to take a teaching post or get a job in a factory. In the event she was sent to Le Puy, a picturesque little town set among the volcanic hills of the Massif Central — it was said, to dim her revolutionary ardour, and get her as far away from Paris as possible.

Le Puy (1931–2)

Before taking up her post, Simone spent a holiday on the Normandy coast, in Reville, where she got to know some of the fishermen and insisted on going out with them in all weathers fishing, hard enough work in calm weather for someone of her slight physique with no experience. She continued the pattern established during her student days of combining physical and intellectual effort, by teaching the fishermen mathematics during rest periods and explaining the Catechism to the daughter of one of them. The fishermen seem to have been greatly impressed by her capacity for hard work, by her gifts as a teacher, and by her real desire to live like them, and defended her against the charges of Communism brought against her by some of the other holiday-makers.

Later that summer she returned to Paris for a conference of the C G T, the *Confédération Générale du Travail*, a trade union with which she was to have a somewhat stormy relationship for the next few years. After that she went down to Le Puy to install herself before the start of the new school year. Her mother went with her, to help her settle in, as she was to do for all her subsequent teaching posts. Knowing that her daughter would deny herself even the basics of existence, and would in any case have her mind on things other than her own comfort, she tried to make sure that she had fuel to heat herself with, gave her flat-mate instructions as to what Simone could and could not eat, and after her departure sent food parcels at regular intervals to ensure that she would not starve. It was to no avail: Simone refused consistently to be organised, and gently but firmly rejected her mother's efforts. She had decided to live on the starting salary of a primary-school teacher, whereas her qualifications entitled her to a good deal more; all the rest was distributed among various causes, unemployment funds, strike funds and suchlike. She disliked individual charity, though since she deliberately left money lying around her room, with the door open, sometimes it would disappear, to her total unconcern. Mostly she did not even realise: as far as she was concerned, money should be like water, finding its own level and flowing to where there was none. She was not conscious of giving, because she was not conscious of possessing. A simple law of justice regarding those that had and those that had not governed her actions.

It was in this spirit that she became involved with the unemployed in Le Puy. These were difficult days for working people in France, and in Europe generally. The Wall Street Crash of 1929 had been the signal for the economic depression of the 1930s. Industrial production went down in France by 17 per cent in 1931 — in the case of steel production it was 29 per cent — creating inevitably a great deal of unemployment. In Le Puy, as elsewhere, this situation caused a lot of hardship. The unemployed, who were without any form of benefit, were given jobs stone-breaking for the miserable wage of 6 francs a day for those who managed to work fast enough, as they were paid by volume and were obviously not experienced at the job. Simone soon associated herself with their cause and, on one occasion, accompanied a delegation to the Mayor's office, and subsequently to a municipal council meeting, to make their grievances known. Because they were at one point letting themselves be intimidated by the more articulate officials, she spoke up for them and put their case. This caused an uproar in the locality. The newspapers took up the story, wildly distorting both Simone's behaviour and the incident as a whole. She for her part not only did not back down, but took an obvious delight in provoking local conservative opinion by letting herself be seen in the company of the unemployed, actually on occasion shaking hands with them and entering a café in their company. To the rigid sense of hierarchy of the good bourgeois of Le Puy, such behaviour was profoundly shocking. Simone was widely believed to be a Communist, and did nothing to dispel the illusion, striding around Le Puy with a copy of the Communist newspaper, *L'Humanité*, under her arm. The affair rumbled on; Simone had the distinction of being preached against in the cathedral, but also the support of her pupils at the *lycée* and their parents, who organised a petition, and that of the various unions with which she was involved, both professionally and otherwise. The school administration was clearly highly embarrassed by the whole business: they did not want a confrontation, but hated scandal. Simone was offered a post in an industrial town — probably St-Quentin — if she would sign an application for transfer, which she refused, saying she had started the year there, and would finish it. Her teaching, however, came under strict scrutiny, and more attention than usual was paid to the routine inspection for teachers beginning in the profession. To be fair to the inspector, he appreciated the work she was doing with her class, but predicted that only two pupils would pass their *baccalauréat* at the end of the year, a prediction which turned out to be entirely accurate.

This was largely because of her unconventional approach to the syllabus. In her teaching methods she followed largely the methods used by Alain, depending on the classics of literature — Balzac, Tolstoy and so forth — as much as on Plato and Kant in her philosophy classes. She encouraged the pupils to write as much as possible, and sought to awaken their critical responses rather than to feed them ready-made ideas of the sort to be found in the manuals of philosophy then in use. Although her commitment to her own ideas was clearly strong, the petition organised by the parents of her pupils speaks of the impartiality of her teaching. In spite of her lack of obvious pedagogic skills — her teaching was characterised by a certain physical awkwardness, and a monotonous delivery — her pupils held her in considerable esteem, and had great affection for her. This was a common reaction to her teaching: most of her pupils, both those she taught formally in the classroom, and the many individuals she undertook to coach at various times in her career, were conscious of an irresistible moral presence, which uplifted them in spite of themselves, and of an ability to place herself on the level of any student, however humble or however gifted.

The affair with the unemployed did not exhaust her capacity for social involvement. Not too far to the east of Le Puy — though still in those days three hours away by train — was the mining town of St-Etienne, and soon Simone had made contact with people involved in the trade union movement there, in particular Urbain and Albertine Thévenon, with whom she was to develop a close friendship. In the circle of syndicalist teachers of which Urbain Thévenon was a leading figure, Simone felt completely at home, sharing their refusal to become fashionable 'intellectuals' in the French tradition. Her subsequent relationships with working-class figures such as Pierre Monatte and Marcel Martinet were based on the same refusal to set herself apart from those whose cause she espoused. At St-Etienne she quickly became involved in syndicalist activity, working with others to bring about a union between the C G T and the C G T U (the *Confédération Générale du Travail Unitaire*). The latter, of Communist inspiration, had been born from the divisions of 1922, but from 1924 was no more than an instrument of party propaganda among the working classes. The much larger C G T was composed by the 1930s of many State employees, minor civil servants, teachers and the like, but also of miners, who were of reformist tendency. But the existence of the two opposing union groupings made for weakness in the movement, and in fact it proved almost entirely ineffectual during the 1930s. Simone, however, at this time believed strongly in the possibility of social change through union action, and devoted much time and energy to the furtherance of union activity in St-Etienne. She wrote numerous articles for *L'Effort* (the newspaper of the *Cartel Autonome du Bâtiment de Lyon*, the building workers' union), and found in the mining community a sense of fraternity to which she was deeply sensitive. She became involved again with workers' education, this time through the Workers' Colleges organised by Thévenon. As before, she was concerned above all to give working people the tools with which they could liberate themselves from the hold of intellectuals of all kinds — herself included, of course. She followed Marx in his desire to abolish 'the degrading division of intellectual and manual work'. To this end, Simone took upon herself a class in the French language as being a primary tool in the liberation process, and shared with Thévenon a class in political economics.

All this was inevitably a great strain on her none-too-robust health. She had her teaching at the *lycée*, which she prepared very fully and conscientiously, giving extra time when necessary to her pupils; she was involved in union activities at Le Puy and committed to exhausting journeys to and from St-Etienne, frequently losing a night's sleep as she did so, in order to take part in union business there and give her classes for the miners. She found time to write numerous articles which, although circumstantial, are nevertheless well-documented. In addition, she was suffering from headaches during the whole of this period, sometimes so bad that she could not eat for several days, and went to her classes only to have her pupils read aloud to her, as she held her head in her hands. At the end of the year she asked to be transferred to St-Etienne, but this was refused. She was sent instead to Auxerre, a town in the Yonne, to the south-east of Paris.

Auxerre (1932–3)

Before taking up her post, she made a visit to Germany, which she had been wanting to do for some time. In Germany in the early 1930s, the situation was tense: the National Socialists under Hitler were gaining ground all the time, and there was a steady upsurge of anti-Communist, anti-trade union and anti-Jewish sentiment which was making life increasingly difficult for large numbers of people, although Hitler had not as yet consolidated his power. Simone wanted to see the situation at first hand, although she was warned of the potential danger of her visit by various friends who knew the situation. She went nevertheless, and her first letters home from Berlin report all quiet, in an attempt to reassure her family and friends. Her parents were not convinced, however, and promptly set out to join her. Some of her time in Germany was therefore spent with them.

Her subsequent letters, which were developed into extensive articles on her return, give her impressions in detail. She speaks of the contagiousness of the Nazi ideology which, however, did not seem at that stage to affect relationships between individuals. She is full of admiration for young German workers, dynamic, courageous and intelligent, with a level of culture far surpassing that of their French counterparts. What concerns and finally scandalises her most is the total lack of opposition to Hitler: the Communist Party had simply capitulated before the rising tide of Nazism, and had further weakened opposition on the Left by their doctrinaire refusal to join forces with the Social Democrats. Faced with their capitulation, Simone admits to having lost any respect she ever had for the Communists, and predicts a catastrophic situation for Germany in the near future.

In her early days in Auxerre she developed these ideas into articles for various journals. The situation in Germany evolved very fast and before the last of the articles appeared her predictions had come true. In January 1933 Hitler became Chancellor. The burning of the Reichstag on 27 February gave him an opportunity to clamp down even more harshly on dissident elements, and the elections of 5 March gave a huge majority to the Nazis. It only remained for Hitler to seek and obtain supreme power from the Reichstag on 23 March, and the mechanism was set up that would eventually lead to the Second World War.

Simone's articles on Germany were heavily criticised by the Communist Left, who felt that she had betrayed them, but she was supported by figures of note such as Boris Souvarine, whom she came to know at this time. He was a founder member of the French Communist Party, a Russian *émigré* and Communist dissident who was at this time still Marxist-Leninist, but who was to emerge as one of Stalin's greatest detractors. On meeting, Simone and Souvarine experienced a mutual admiration for one another, and a warm friendship developed. He was certainly one of the people to whom she was closest at that time, and she continued until her death to be deeply sensitive to his opinion of her. Their uncompromising concern for the truth in the interpretation of contemporary events, and their common sense of betrayal at the course of the Revolution in Russia, made for a meeting of like minds.

Meanwhile, Simone was settling into her new teaching post. Whereas in Le Puy relationships with the administration had been uneasy, here they were frankly bad from the start. She seemed to experience a total antipathy towards the *lycée*, turned her back on the headmistress when spoken to, spent any staff meetings she was obliged to attend reading the newspaper and smoking, but otherwise ignoring everybody. Why she should have taken provocation to these lengths is difficult to tell: certainly she gave no one a chance to form a relationship with her. Her philosophy class gave her little satisfaction: Auxerre was a military base, and she had a number of officers' daughters in the class. They were well-behaved, apparently, but according to her they refused to be involved in ideas, everything ran straight off them, and she felt she was getting nowhere. She tried to have them experiment with a small printing-press, which she obtained for them to print their own essays, but the pupils objected that this made their hands dirty, so she gave up the experiment. Her annual inspection predicted poor results, and the prediction proved accurate. At the end of the year, the headmistress, unable to contemplate a further year with Simone, simply suppressed the philosophy post, and Simone was on the move again, this time to Roanne.

Roanne (1933–4)

The year which Simone spent in Roanne was one in which she became more and more alienated from the trade unions, less and less sympathetic to the French Communist Party, and more and more critical of Russia and fearful of what was going on in Germany. Given these preoccupations, it was natural that she should spend the long summer break before taking up her post in Roanne firstly seeing her old friends in St-Etienne, where she gave lectures on the events in Germany, and then in Rheims, for a union conference, where she took issue with the Communists over the attitude of the U S S R to German refugees, who were being refused right of entry. At the same time a major article of hers, 'Perspectives: allons-nous vers la révolution prolétarienne?' ('Prospects: are we heading for the proletarian revolution?') (*OL* 9–38)[3] came out in the periodical *La Révolution Prolétarienne*. In it she bitterly criticised the failure of the Russian Revolution, the defeat of the German workers' movement, and the conflicts and the impotence of the French unions. On a theoretical level, she criticised Marx for his failure to predict accurately the way history would evolve: instead of capitalist oppression being replaced by the dictatorship of the proletariat, it was another form of oppression, that of the bureaucratic State, which had taken its place. The article was greatly admired by Souvarine among others, who felt that it was one of her best political pieces, but criticised angrily by the traditional Left, who found it too pessimistic. It is true that by this time Simone did not have much confidence in the ability of the Left to bring about a more just society.

Around this time also she wrote a review of Rosa Luxemburg's *Letters from Prison*, which is interesting for the particular characteristics of this militant figure that she emphasises. Whereas there is a tendency to see Simone Weil as dolorist in her obsession with the sufferings of humanity, in this review she underlines the joy and love of life that Rosa manifests. The letters, she says, demonstrate 'an aspiration to life and not to death, to effective action and not to sacrifice'. She sees in her the genuine pagan and Stoic spirit, in that she was at home in the universe, independent of the events that occurred in it.

In September Simone attended the C G T U conference in Paris, but was effectively prevented from speaking. All non-

Communist elements were suppressed.

The year in Roanne was a much better one from the teaching point of view. Her philosophy class was small, with only four or five pupils, and had a family feeling about it. One of her pupils, Anne Reynaud, kept and eventually published her notes,[4] and from these it is possible to see how Simone prolonged the reflection of her master Alain, in certain areas, while developing in an original way aspects of social and political philosophy. In the *lycée* in general she seemed on much better terms with the administration, though she occasionally crossed swords with the headmistress, who would come looking for marks and rankings which Simone generally refused to give.

At Christmas Simone went home to Paris. There she persuaded her parents to put up Trotsky in their flat, since he was in Paris looking for somewhere to hold a — semi-clandestine — meeting. The visit was the occasion for a long confrontation between Trotsky and Simone, who disagreed on nearly everything. At the end Trotsky, exasperated and uncomprehending, asked her: 'Why do you put me up? Are you the Salvation Army?'

Simone was, if fact, more and more pessimistic over the political situation in France and elsewhere. In a letter to a former pupil at Le Puy, she predicts the future in sombre tones: 'We are at the beginning of a period of dictatorship more centralised and more oppressive than anything we have known in history. . . . One fine day (maybe we shall live to see it, maybe we shan't), everything will collapse in anarchy, and we will return to almost primitive forms of struggle for existence'.[5] In the meantime, syndicalist activity was to less and less purpose. One could not look to Russia since, as she says in another letter to the same pupil, 'in no country [. . .] are the working masses more wretched, more oppressed, more debased than in Russia'.[6]

Given this situation, with so many spheres of action closed, and yet so urgent a need to do something, she resolved to devote all her energies henceforth to two causes: the maintenance of peace, and the colonial question. She did not, however, cut herself off from all her previous contacts: although disillusioned with syndicalism, she spent a good deal of time during the year in Roanne at St-Etienne, where she had excellent relationships with the miners. She also found herself increasingly giving assistance to refugees from Hitler's Germany, sometimes with money to enable them to survive, sometimes enlisting the help of her parents to put them up in the spare flat they had, overlooking the Luxembourg Gardens in Paris.

At the same time she was working on what she referred to in ironic tones as her 'Great Work', or her 'Testament', a major essay entitled 'Réflexions sur les causes de la liberté et de l'oppression sociale'('Reflections on the causes of liberty and oppression in society') (*OL* 55 – 162),[7] in which she analyses the way in which man has freed himself from the tyranny of nature only to enslave himself to his fellow-man in the work-situation. Work is the central theme of this essay, her main preoccupation being to find a means of production in a modern context which does not enslave the worker through depriving him of his capacity for thought and for decision-making.

It is clear that the theory and practice of work were preoccupying her more and more at this time. And yet she felt increasingly that she was writing about something which she had not studied in practice, which she had not experienced at first hand.[8] Accordingly, at the end of the academic year she resolved to put into effect a project which she had nursed ever since her time at the Ecole Normale, and take a job in a factory for a period of time. She requested leave of absence 'for personal studies', saying that she wanted to prepare a thesis on the relationship between modern technology, which is the basis for industry, and essential aspects of our civilisation, i.e. social organisation and culture. Although the desire to experience factory conditions at first hand was obviously important to her, she did indeed want to 'study', as she had indicated, and assure the theoretical basis to her thinking. In fact, she did not enter factory life until December 1934, spending the autumn completing the 'Great Work'.

Factory Work

Although there is a clear continuity in both Simone Weil's life and her thinking, the months she spent working in a factory were a watershed. In the autobiographical letter to Father Perrin to which I have already referred, she recalls her state of mind immediately afterwards, and notes:

> This contact with affliction had killed my youth. [...] I knew very well that there was a great deal of affliction in the world, I was obsessed by it, but I had never become aware of it through prolonged contact. In the factory, [...] other people's affliction entered my flesh and my soul. [...] It was there that I was branded for ever as a slave. . . .[9]

This new sensitivity opened her to certain experiences, particularly those of a spiritual nature: the first contact with Christianity which 'really counted' took place immediately after her months in the factory, and it is clear that her physical and moral state at that time played a large part in the way she interpreted it. Beforehand, she had had a general sympathy towards certain religious ideas: afterwards, she was receptive to the experience itself. What she underwent in the factory matured her emotionally and spiritually, and because to understand was always for her to understand experience, it also made her more aware intellectually. As a person she therefore matured: in particular, the harshness of some of her earlier reactions was modified. In addition, a sombre note was struck which never again left her. We should not forget, of course, the state of Europe at this time and until her death: in 1936 the Spanish Civil War broke out, leading almost directly into the World War in 1939, in both of which Simone Weil was deeply involved. There was, therefore, more than enough to cause her anguish in these years.

Although we can speak of the factory experience being a watershed, it would be wrong to see a rupture between what went before and after. It is certainly a mistake to create a militant/mystic opposition on either side of the factory experience. Her political activity continued throughout: the militant syndicalism of the earlier period was simply replaced by her abandonment of pacifism and her involvement in the war situation. Some of her most profound and pertinent political writings are post-factory experience. Furthermore, we have seen how, even in her period of political militancy, she was not fundamentally hostile to religious ideas.

It is clear, however, that the factory was a shattering experience for her, and we should perhaps ask now why it should have been so. The first point to note is that many of Simone Weil's observations on factory work are objectively totally accurate: the factory was only too often in the 1930s an exhausting, dangerous and soul-destroying environment. The Depression had created a situation where factory bosses could hire and fire more or less as they pleased, because jobs were scarce, and any worker who did not please for any reason could easily be replaced. At the same time they were under great economic pressure, and were reluctant to pay more than the basic minimum necessary to keep production going. 'Taylorisation', the system imported from the United States, whereby the rhythms of work are studied in order to get the maximum possible production out of a given worker, had a total hold over French management, and the rigid hierarchy established between skilled and unskilled meant that every group despised the one beneath it. Fraternity, the sense of corporate effort, was almost impossible in such a context.

We must also, however, consider the situation of Simone Weil herself in such an environment. There was perhaps never anyone less suited to factory work. Physically slight, she had none of the muscular wiriness sometimes associated with that physique. Her hands were disproportionately small, and were devoid of any kind of dexterity. She was clumsy and absent-minded, as well as short-sighted, which made approaching any kind of machinery a hazardous undertaking. Years of excessive discipline towards an already frail body had depleted her physical resources: the punishing work-routine she had imposed on herself since student days and the meagre nourishment she had allowed herself had taken their inevitable toll. She was subject to constant blinding headaches of a kind that would have incapacitated lesser beings. Intellectually, she was conditioned to want to understand everything she did, and to have control over her actions and her environment, and was totally unsuited to the grinding and mindless repetition involved in factory work.

Do these factors effectively falsify her impressions? In one sense yes, in that she had not already had all human response deadened out of her by early conditioning. She lived totally on her wages, however, in constant fear of dismissal and unemployment, and her imaginative grasp of situations was such that her life as a bourgeois intellectual was to all intents and purposes forgotten. Life on the production line or on the shop-floor was so soul-destroying, so physically exhausting, that in any case most days she had no energy left to think. She might have misread some of the reactions of her fellow-workers, but she could not misread the accidents she witnessed, the cut fingers, the woman half-scalped by getting her hair caught in a machine, who was back on the job the same day.

At a time of high unemployment, Simone might have had difficulty getting employment in the first place, given that she had no previous experience. The fact that she was able to do so was largely through the good offices of Souvarine, who put her in touch with Auguste Detœuf, the enlightened and thoughtful administrator of the Société Alsthom, which specialised in the manufacture of electrical parts. He was persuaded to take Simone on in one of his factories in the rue Lecourbe, and there she started in December as a factory hand, working first on a drilling machine, and then on a power press. She kept a detailed record of her experiences and impressions, in a 'Journal d'usine' ('Factory Journal'), published as part of *La Condition ouvrière* (*CO* 35–107).[10] After the Christmas break, when she was laid off, she was put on the furnaces where, in addition to the necessity to work at speed, there was the hazard of burns, and the heavy manual work of raising and lowering the furnace door. Piece-work was torture to her: the submission of every movement to the necessity to go faster, because you were paid for what you did, and if you did not go fast enough you did not eat, was unbearable. By the middle of January, exhausted, she succumbed to an ear infection, and was off work for a month. She returned towards the end of February, coping reasonably well at first, but soon exhaustion and her headaches returned, and she was almost relieved to be laid off for a week. Early in April she left Alsthom definitively, though whether she was laid off or decided to quit is not clear. Fairly quickly she found work again, however, this time at the Forges de Basse-Indre, at Boulogne-Billancourt in the Paris suburbs. She was put on a press cutting out parts, where the rhythm was impossible and the foreman a bully. When she could not keep up the necessary pace she was moved to another machine inserting metal bands, and from there into a separate workshop where, for the first time, the workers had time to exchange an occasional word. A woman whom she engaged in conversation on the way home told her that after a certain time, maybe a year, you learned not to suffer. Simone thought that that was the last stage of degradation.

After a month at Boulogne-Billancourt, Simone was again dismissed, and for the next month was unemployed, living only on her unemployment benefit, which was meagre. She eventually found a job with Renault, and was put on a milling-machine. She seems to have coped with the work-rhythm better here, and was kept on after her trial period of one month. However, she was a victim of two accidents which needed medical attention, and it was only an intense effort of will that got her to work every day. She was a constant prey to the arbitrary orders and rebukes of the foremen, and it was probably after some such incident that, getting into the bus in the evening, she suddenly had the strange feeling that she, as a slave, had no right to be carrying out such an ordinary action. The slavery of the factory process had made her lose all sense of having any rights, so that any moment when she did not have to submit to the brutality of her fellow-beings seemed like a special favour.

In August she left the factory. She had decided that she had learned what she needed to know, and had asked for a teaching post for 1935–6. Looking back on the experience, she found that she had acquired the feeling of having absolutely no rights, but also the capacity for being endlessly humiliated without being humiliated in her own eyes. Every day the feeling of human dignity had been broken in her, and she whose whole concern had been to understand what she was doing had been obliged constantly to submit to another's orders, to be manipulated as an object instead of thinking for herself. To her great surprise, her reaction had been one not of revolt, but of submission.

Portugal, Bourges (1935–6)

In this state of complete exhaustion, physical and moral, Simone Weil went for a holiday to Portugal with her parents. It was there that she had the first of the 'three contacts with Christianity which really counted'. She recounts the experience in the autobiographical letter to Father Perrin:

> My parents had taken me to Portugal, and I left them to go alone to a little village.[11][. . .] In a wretched physical state, I went into this little Portuguese village which was, alas, very

wretched too, alone, one evening at the full moon, on their saint's day. [...] The fishermen's wives were processing around the boats, carrying candles, and singing songs which were certainly very ancient, and of heartrending sadness. [...] There I suddenly became convinced that Christianity is the religion of slaves *par excellence*, that slaves cannot help belonging to it, I among others.[12]

Immediately after this, Simone set off for Bourges, where again her mother helped to install her. There were probably a dozen pupils in her philosophy class, more sceptical than in her previous posts, but with whom nevertheless she established a good relationship. More and more her teaching revolved around concrete illustrations, still often taken from literary classics, but now often referring, albeit in an indirect way, to her factory experience. Her relationships with the administration in Bourges were on the whole good, as they were with a number of her colleagues. As usual, however, she did not restrict herself to class work. Through one of her pupils she managed to organise herself a visit to the Foundry at Rosières, where she got to know Monsieur Bernard, an engineer and technical director of the factory. She offered him a text for the factory journal, *Entre Nous*, entitled 'Un appel aux ouvriers de R[osières]'('An appeal to the workers at Rosières')(*CO* 128–32),[13] in which she asked the workers to write down their impressions of factory work, and expose their sufferings. Monsieur Bernard refused this, believing the article to be provocative and potentially disruptive of a peaceful situation. Simone subsequently wrote and had published there the fine short text on the Greek play, *Antigone* (*SG* 57–62),[14] with a view to making the Greek classics intelligible to working people. She entered into correspondence with Monsieur Bernard, but when the coming to power of the Popular Front government in June brought about a wave of strikes and the occupation of the factories, Simone could not help expressing to Monsieur Bernard her delight at the victory of the workers over the management. Monsieur Bernard, not unnaturally, was upset by this, and the correspondence ended there.

In March of that year she was in contact with a family of peasants in the region, the Bellevilles, with a view to helping them on their small farm. The experiment did not last long, however: although she did everything required of her, and proved quite able at the work, the Bellevilles simply did not understand her, with her everlasting questions and her asceticsm which made her refuse delicacies they offered her, and after a month they asked her to leave. They admitted later that what unnerved them most was her wish to be like them: all the other intellectuals they had come across put up barriers between themselves and the peasants; Simone Weil simply tore them down.

Her health continued to plague her, in particular her headaches, which became so severe that at one point she began to fear total degeneracy. She resolved therefore to take another year off teaching, since she felt she would never understand what she needed to while remaining in the classroom. She investigated the possibility of obtaining a Rockefeller grant, but it seems that she did not in the end pursue this. But in a letter of this period she reveals just how impossible she was finding it to say what she had to say — which she felt contained 'the seeds of great things' — because of her permanent state of poor health. Having left her post in Bourges, however, and before she was able to find the new direction to her life she was seeking, the Spanish Civil War had broken out, in which she immediately became deeply involved.

The Spanish Civil War, Journey to Italy (1936–7)

Spain at this time was led by a Popular Front government, which had come to power following democratic elections in February 1936. The elections had not, however, satisfied the Right, and in particular the Army. In July the Generals, led by Franco, rebelled against the Republican government, and within a matter of days the country was in the grip of a Civil War which quickly spread to all parts. Because it seemed, from the outside at least, a clear case of right-wing privilege opposing a left-wing government which had the interests of the long-oppressed peasantry and the working classes at heart, the conflict was quickly internationalised. The situation was immediately exploited by the rising Fascist powers in Germany and Italy, who sent a large amount of material support to the rebels, and whilst the Republicans had virtually no aid from any other government, particularly at the beginning, their plight caught the imagination of the European

Left, who arrived in Spain in a steady stream throughout the summer of 1936 in order to fight in their support.

When the war broke out, Simone Weil was in Paris. In the past she had been totally identified with the pacifist cause. Now, hating war as much as ever, she accepted the reality of a war that was actually taking place and, unable to sit back in safety in Paris while others were being killed, promptly joined the ranks of those crossing the border into Spain. This involved no conflict with her anti-war sentiments, as far as she was concerned: she in fact continued to write pacifist articles and support the pacifist cause on her return. But her pacifism was based not so much on a repugnance to kill, a repugnance which she recognised most people shared, but on the realisation that war in Europe was simply the greatest possible evil, and must be avoided at all costs. She was in this respect similar to countless other Frenchmen, in whom the catastrophe of the First World War had created a horror of war in general, and a determination that it should never happen again. She approved Léon Blum's non-intervention policy in Spain, wanting him in fact to go further and maintain a pacifist position against Hitler, instead of threatening to intervene.

Simone Weil enlisted in the Republican forces, therefore, and joined Durruti's Anarchist column. The first task that she volunteered for was refused her: Maurin, the founder of the POUM, the *Partido obrero de unificación marxista*, and a brother-in-law of Souvarine, had disappeared behind enemy lines, and Simone offered to go and try to find him. It was evidently considered too hazardous an undertaking, though, and she was not allowed to go. As the Spanish Civil War was a rehearsal for the Second World War, so Simone's frustrations here were a foretaste of the much greater frustrations she was to experience between 1939 and her death in 1943. At every point she had to insist on being included in the action. She had a rifle, and was obviously prepared to use it if necessary, as she asked someone to charge it for her.

Ironically, she met her fate not on the field of battle, but in the kitchen, where she was being used somewhat against her will. Her short sight prevented her from seeing a large pan of boiling oil on the floor, and she put her foot in it, burning it badly. Although she was hospitalised, the burn was inadequately treated, and on the arrival of her parents who, characteristically, had set out in a desperate attempt to track her down, she was taken back to France where the wound slowly began to heal.

This accident took her out of a situation with which she had been becoming rapidly more and more disillusioned. She was appalled at the atrocities on both sides — she was one of the few committed witnesses to see wrongs in her own camp. Another was Georges Bernanos, to whom she wrote some time later when she read his *Les Grands Cimetières sous la lune*, an account of the reign of terror which the Fascists under Franco imposed on Majorca. Bernanos was a Catholic, and a Royalist, and could have been expected to sympathise rather with the Fascist rebels, but he was as revolted by their crimes as Simone was by those of the Republicans. She congratulates him in her letter, saying that because of his capacity to denounce evil wherever it was found, he was infinitely closer to her than the Anarchists with whom she was fighting.

Debilitated by both the accident and her general physical condition, Simone was on sick-leave for the whole of the academic year 1936–7. She attended some syndicalist meetings, though with little enthusiasm, as she was frequently critical of their policies. She undertook a report on a series of strikes in Lille, in which she exposes worker abuses as well as management intransigence. In her view, slavery had disappeared from the factories in Lille, only to be replaced by disorder and anarchy. It was a matter of some urgency, therefore, to find a new order.

Towards the end of April she was well enough to travel to Italy for a visit which lasted until mid-June, a period which was to prove one of the happiest and most enriching of her adult life. Her purpose was partly holiday, but partly that which had taken her to Germany: foreseeing catastrophe, she wanted to see the situation from the inside. During the month preceding the visit, she underwent treatment for her headaches at a clinic at Montana, and there she met a young medical student, Jean Posternak, with whom she struck up a friendship. It is through her letters to him that we learn of her experiences in Italy, in particular her immense pleasure in discovering the artistic life there. She was spellbound by Florence, the Medici chapel, the bridges on the Arno, the Uffizi and the Pizzi galleries, San Miniato. . . . However, she makes lively comment also on the people she met, even though her conversation was limited by her Italian. She visited the opera several times — to hear Mozart, Rossini, and Verdi (whom she did not like) — but also heard Whitsuntide liturgical music at St Peter's in Rome. Her visit to Assisi and the surrounding countryside captivated her in every way: she tells Posternak that everything else paled before the Franciscan landscape. It was also in Assisi that she had the second of the significant contacts with Christianity, although it was only in 1942 that she recounted it in her letter to Father Perrin. Neither Posternak nor her parents learned of it at the time: 'There, being alone in the little twelfth-century Romanesque chapel of Santa Maria degli Angeli, that incomparable marvel of purity, where St Francis often prayed, something stronger than myself made me, for the first time in my life, go down on my knees'.[15]

Simone returned to France just before the resignation of Léon Blum on 23 June, and the end of the Popular Front government. Simone had always appreciated Blum's intelligence and the inspiration of his social policies, but felt that his failure was due to his incapacity to use the state of the popular imagination on his coming to power in order to take certain economic measures. Blum lacked political intelligence: a true politician knows how to use the collective imagination to act on social conditions, without sharing the illusions of the collective.

By this time Simone was feeling well enough to apply for another teaching post, and for the new academic year was sent to St-Quentin, an industrial town to the north-east of Paris, a post which had attracted her since her year at Le Puy.

St-Quentin and the Approach of War (1937–9)

In fact Simone was to teach here only for one term, since by January her headaches were so bad that she had again to apply for sick-leave for the rest of the academic year, which was subsequently prolonged into the next. It was effectively the end of teaching for her, because by the time she was able to apply again for a post, the war and the German occupation of France had intervened, and by her Jewish origins she was excluded from teaching.

Being now closer to Paris, she travelled there frequently for meetings of the *Nouveaux Cahiers*, a study group founded in 1936 by Auguste Detœuf, for whom she had worked at Alsthom. The group, consisting of Detœuf and other enlightened industrialists and interested parties, founded the review *Les Nouveaux Cahiers* in 1937, in which Simone published several articles. The members met weekly to discuss some topic of social concern: Simone had already attended some of their meetings while in Bourges, but now went more frequently. From the records it is clear that, when Germany was discussed, she was still not prepared to face war to destroy Hitler. Even at the time of the Anschluss in March, when Hitler annexed Austria, Simone's response was to call again for negotiation, to prevent the slide into war.

Other matters preoccupying her at this time included increasingly the colonial question. She wrote an article defending Messali Hadj, the Algerian patriot who had been sentenced to two years in prison for having tried to resurrect under a different name the *Etoile nord-africaine*, an organisation founded by Messali Hadj and banned by the first Popular Front government, and which enjoyed a good deal of support among Algerian workers in France. Simone knew Messali Hadj personally, and it seems she may have approached Léon Blum at one point on his behalf, before his arrest.

The colonial question and the increasingly tense situation in Europe are brought together in a letter she wrote to Gaston Bergery, replying to an article on Czechoslovakia which he had written in his review *La Flèche*. Simone considered that both allowing Hitler to annex the German Sudeten, who formed part of Czechoslovakia, and opposing him in his designs, could lead to war, but that the first option was less likely to do so. What was clear to her was that an all-out war in Europe would be a certain catastrophe, whereas a German hegemony in Europe, however bitter a prospect, would not necessarily be a total evil. She links this to the colonial question, adding that for France to lose part of her independence would be less shameful than to continue to oppress and exploit Arabs, Indochinese and other colonial peoples. One feels here the conflict between her strong patriotism, her need to identify with the policies and political acts of her country, and the shame which her lucid appraisal of these policies caused her. The acuteness of the conflict seems to have been an important factor in her underestimation of the Nazi menace as demonstrated in this letter, and the ultimately short-sighted judgements she expresses in it are certainly among those she regretted later when war had broken out.

At Easter, Simone went to Solesmes to hear the particularly fine Gregorian chant sung by the monks of the Abbey there. She had become increasingly drawn to this form of liturgical music: prior to her visit to Italy the previous year she had gone to Einsiedeln, probably at Easter, precisely to hear the chant. At Solesmes she followed all the services from Palm Sunday to Easter Tuesday. Her headaches were by this time excruciating but, as she later wrote to Father Perrin, by an extreme effort of attention she was able to dissociate herself from her suffering body and immerse herself totally in the pure beauty of the liturgy. 'It goes without saying', she wrote, 'that in the course of these services the thought of the Passion of Christ entered into me for good.'[16]

There was at Solesmes a young Englishman, John Vernon, who introduced her to the English Metaphysical poets of the seventeeth century. In the letter to Perrin she describes how later, probably around November of that year, she discovered the poem by George Herbert entitled 'Love' and, finding it particularly beautiful, learned it by heart. She took to reciting it when her headaches were particularly bad, giving it her total and undivided attention. At first, she says, she thought she was simply reciting a beautiful poem: but unknown to her it had the virtue of a prayer. 'It was while I was reciting it once that [. . .] Christ himself came down and took me.'[17]

I will return to this experience at a later stage, but several points can be made about it here. Firstly, the experience was totally unexpected. She was not seeking to provoke a mystical experience, indeed, as she herself said, she had never read the mystics,[18] and other people's accounts of mystical encounters had always repelled her rather than anything else. A person-to-person contact between God and man had never occurred to her as a real possibility. The experience was unlikely therefore to be a result of suggestion. Although increasingly interested in religious questions she was not a Catholic. Her whole background and training had taught her to be sceptical of this kind of experience, and her total commitment to the truth as something extra-personal would make her very wary of what would seem on the face of it to be a subjective experience. In addition, she states quite clearly that neither her senses nor her imagination played any part in it. It was thus as unlike a human encounter as possible, although Simone, in describing it, has recourse inevitably to terms evocative of a human relationship: she felt the presence of a love analogous to that which you read 'in the smile on the face of a loved one'. Suffering also played a role in the experience: here, as elsewhere, physical suffering, affliction, becomes one of the paths to a contact with supernatural reality.

Her physical suffering was certainly intense at this time. Her headaches became so bad that she feared a tumour, and consulted yet another specialist, prepared for the worst. But he again was unable to diagnose anything. Her physical and moral state was such, however, that, as she recounts in a letter to the poet Joë Bousquet, she began to ask herself whether death was not for her the most imperative of duties, and resolved on suicide, but conditionally and after a fixed lapse of time.

Meanwhile on the political front the menace was growing. The end of September saw the Munich conference, which marked the climax to the policy of appeasement of Hitler led by Britain under Chamberlain, but acquiesced in by France. By giving Hitler all he wanted in a supposed 'settlement' of the Czech question, the Allies thought they were buying peace: in fact they were heading straight for war. Simone's reaction to Munich was one of anxiety: she felt that war had perhaps been deferred, but not prevented. A further step towards war was taken in March 1939, when Hitler invaded Czechoslovakia. Simone, like most people, was dismayed; she seems to have regarded Hitler's act as a turning-point, but still felt that negotiations were not entirely useless, seeing in war and the consequences of war the ultimate catastrophe. She was soon to reproach herself bitterly for what she saw as her short-sightedness, but for the moment her pacifism seems to have outweighed all other considerations.

The War: Marseilles

In September 1939 the inevitable happened, and war was declared. The Weil family were at Nice at the time, but returned immediately to Paris. Simone's immediate reaction was that, now war was a reality, it was imperative to give maximum support to Britain in the struggle. It is interesting, however, that the question of France's own moral standing was still uppermost in her mind. In an article she wrote at the time, she declares that it is insufficient in both moral and strategic terms to be simply less brutal, less violent, less inhuman than the enemy: on the contrary, it is necessary to manifest the opposing virtues in order to stand up to the enemy. Moreover, those virtues are lacking while France continues to oppress its colonial peoples. The same sentiments are expressed in a letter which she wrote to the writer Jean Giraudoux around the same time, reacting to a radio broadcast he had made in which he had claimed that the French Empire was attached to France by bonds other than those of subordination and exploitation. Simone in her letter wishes with all her heart it were so, and gives instances of brutality, physical and moral, in the relationships between France and her colonies.

From now on, all Simone's activity was concerned more or less with the war. In the early months she wrote the fine essay *'L'Iiade ou le poème de la force'* (*'The Iliad* or the poem of force') (*SG* 11–42),[19] under the pseudonym of Emile Novis, and also the three-part 'Quelques réflexions sur les origines de l'hitlérisme' ('Some reflections on the origins of Hitlerism') (*EH* 11–60).[20] In the latter articles she is already going further than the immediate war situation in an attempt to analyse how the phenomenon of Hitler had been allowed to happen. She sees the origins of his prestige in the state of European society in the years leading up to the war, and concludes that what is necessary is to change society so that neither his nor any other attempt at universal domination could succeed. The major part of these articles is, however, devoted to a long comparison between Hitler's Germany and Ancient Rome — one of the principal models for our society, and one which we are supposed to admire.

The Weils were very concerned for the safety of their son André in the early months of the war. In Finland on a scientific mission when the war broke out, he had been arrested as a spy, deported to Sweden, and subsequently sent back to France. His pacifist position, however, which Simone accused herself of having helped foster, meant that he was immediately imprisoned, first in Le Havre, then in Rouen. The family were allowed to visit him, and in addition Simone wrote a number of long letters to her brother, in which she discusses mainly matters of scientific interest, and which give a clear idea of her views on science, particularly the contrast between Greek science and its modern counterpart.

In the meantime she was elaborating projects to help in the fight against Hitler. The first was a project for helping the Czechs, whereby troops and arms would be parachuted into the country. She submitted this plan to various authorities, insisting that, were it to be put into action, she must be a part of that action. It was obviously shelved in the end, as nothing more was heard of it. The second was a plan, which she was to try in vain to the end of her life to get adopted, for the development and deployment of a squad of front-line nurses, who would go into the firing line to give immediate first aid and comfort the wounded and dying. She again insisted that she must be one of the nurses. She presented this plan to numerous officials, often using well-placed friends to act as intermediaries, while she was still in Marseilles, in New York and in London, but no one could be persuaded of its practicality. De Gaulle himself was reported to have seen it, and to have commented: 'She's mad'.

For eight months, during the Phoney War, little happened in military terms. Then on 10 May, with the return of the fine weather, Hitler began his offensive against Belgium and Holland, which were overrun within days, and from there marched on into France. On 12 June Paris was declared an 'open city' — the Germans entered two days later. Simone at first thought that Paris would be defended and wanted to stay. She was eventually persuaded that any struggle would be taking place elsewhere, and left with her family, carrying only what they had on them, firstly for Nevers, where they thought a new line of defence might be created, then for Vichy, then Toulouse, and finally, in September, Marseilles, where they were to spend the next year. In the meantime, however, on 25 June, the Armistice was signed, signifying the end of hostilities and one of the most traumatic moments in the history of modern France. The great French Army was routed, its leaders totally incompetent to deal with the German advance — although Simone was always to insist that the whole nation bore responsibility for the capitulation. The immediate practical effect of the Armistice was the division of France into two zones, the occupied zone to the north and west, and the so-called free zone, administered from Vichy by a puppet regime under Maréchal Pétain, to the south. The terms of the Armistice were harsh and humiliating for France both morally and materially, effectively obliging France to pay for the war Germany was continuing to wage against Britain.

Simone reacted with horror and outrage to the Armistice, feeling total shame at the capitulation of her country, and convinced that France should have stayed in the war. The rest of the war is the story of her futile search for a way of participating in it in real terms, and her death in large measure the result of the failure of that search. In August, while still in Vichy, she made an application for a teaching post, abroad or in the colonies, feeling that such a move would give her the chance to get to England, where many Frenchmen, including, of course, de Gaulle, had gone in order to carry on the fight. When her application produced no reply, she tried while in Marseilles to get a visa for Portugal, from where she might have been able to get to either Morocco or England.

At the same time she continued to be preoccupied with the colonies for their own sake. She got in touch with the camp at Mazargues in Marseilles where Indochinese workers, brought to France during the 'Phoney War' to work in the factories, were housed. She became indignant at the harsh indifference with which they were treated, and made representations on their behalf to Vichy, denouncing their exploitation. She seems to have had some measure of success, since the camp commandant was subsequently dismissed and replaced by another, after which conditions improved.

She assumed that the silence with which her application for a teaching post had been greeted was a result of her Jewish background, Jews having been banned from all posts in public life under the new Vichy laws. In fact, it seems that she had been offered a post at the *lycée* in Constantine, in Algeria, to begin in October 1940, but due no doubt to the disruptions caused by the war, she never received word of it. She therefore wrote to the Minister of Education asking for clarification of her status. The letter is interesting for the light it throws on the way she saw herself. What is a Jew? she asks. If it is someone practising a particular religion, then she is certainly not one, having been brought up an agnostic, but in a context of Christian civilisation. If it refers to a race, then she cannot imagine that her family, with its Slav origins, has any connection with a people who lived in Palestine two thousand years ago. Rather than a gesture of refusal to identify with the persecuted, this letter can perhaps be seen firstly as a sign of her genuine estrangement from Judaism, with which, rightly or wrongly, she felt she had nothing in common, but also as a refusal to be cut off from suffering humanity in general by being corralled into one particular section of it.

During the time in Marseilles she continued to write intensively. She carried on working on the play, *Venise sauvée*, which she had begun in Vichy, and wrote two important articles on her conception of philosophy. She collaborated with the *Cahiers du Sud*, which published her article on the *Iliad*, and which would subsequently publish her two articles on the Cathars and 'la civilisation d'oc', in which she was becoming increasingly interested. At the same time she read widely in the spiritual literature of India, in particular the *Bhagavad Gītā*, whose message in the context of the war she interpreted as a demonstration of the legitimacy and necessity of action. A few months later she discovered St John of the Cross and read the *Tao-te-Ching* and the *Upanishads*; the nourishment which she derived from these texts is to be found reflected in the Notebooks which she kept at this time.

Her determination to do something practical in the fight against the Nazi occupation was as strong as ever. She soon got in touch with a Resistance network, and had begun working for it, but it turned out to have been infiltrated, and she was picked up and interrogated on a number of occasions. Unable to get anything out of her, one of her interrogators threatened to lock her up with the prostitutes if she did not tell all she knew. To which Simone replied coolly that she would be only too happy, as she had always wanted to get to know that milieu, and could see no way other than prison of doing so. Whereupon the police, convinced she was crazy and that they would get nothing out of her, released her. Later, she was put in touch with Marie-Louise David, and was given an important role in the distribution of the clandestine *Cahiers de Témoignage Chrétien*, one of the more influential Resistance newspapers.

She was also put in touch with Catholic circles in Marseilles, in particular with Father Joseph-Marie Perrin, with whom she had long and frequent conversations between June 1941 and the end of March 1942 on the urgent questions of a spiritual nature which preoccupied her, and on her relationship with the Catholic Church. The latter, which I will consider in more detail at a later stage, caused her acute problems: she admitted in fact that she was more ready to die for the Church than to enter it, since dying implied no lie.

Her physical self-discipline and asceticism were by this time total. She had taken to sleeping on the floor at Nevers, in preparation, she said, for possible future hardship. She ate virtually nothing, because of the real or self-imposed privations of the times, sending most of her ration-tickets to Mazargues and refusing anything she considered a luxury, even when eating with friends. She also refused to queue for anything — except tobacco!

She also decided to exploit her enforced joblessness and fulfil a long-standing desire to become an agricultural worker, extending thus the short periods she had in the past spent on the land. Perrin put her in touch with a friend of his, Gustave Thibon, a self-taught philosopher who farmed in the Ardèche, and in August she began a contact which was soon to become a warm friendship. At the beginning, everything seemed to separate them: Thibon was a Royalist, and a supporter of Vichy, a Catholic with a fine sense of equilibrium who had a natural suspicion of the Jewish left-wing intellectual whom Simone Weil represented. He felt from the start, however, unconditional respect for her integrity, and collaborated fully in her desire to work on the land, although the first few weeks of her stay seem to have been spent reading Greek together. It was as a result of a promise made to Thibon that Simone learnt the Lord's Prayer in Greek, which she took to reciting every morning with total attention. The virtue of this practice was extraordinary, and resulted in experiences of a truly mystical nature. She tells Father Perrin:

> Sometimes the first words already seize my mind and transport it away from my body to a place from where there is neither perspective nor point of view. Space opens. The infinity of the ordinary space of perception is replaced by an infinity to the second or sometimes third power. At the same time, this infinity of infinity fills itself through and through with silence, a silence which is not an absence of sound, and which is the object of a positive sensation, more positive than that of a sound. Sounds, if there are any, only reach me after having crossed this silence.
>
> Sometimes, too, during this recitation or at other moments, Christ is present in person, but with a presence which is

infinitely more real, more poignant, clearer and more filled with love than the first time he took me.[21]

The companionship of Thibon and his family was clearly a great joy to Simone at this time. However, she felt that she was not carrying out her project of becoming an agricultural worker. She therefore got Thibon to persuade a neighbouring winegrower to take her on during the harvest. During the autumn of 1942 she thus did the grape harvest, and took great pride in the fact that she could keep up with the other workers, in spite of her constant headaches and her generally weakened state. She had already formed a plan for the future, to buy a small patch of land in the area, which she and her parents would exploit, getting advice from friends such as Thibon. It came to nothing, since the family left Marseilles shortly afterwards, but it seems to have been a serious project nevertheless. A friend in Marseilles, Hélène Honnorat, once asked her why she should have this urge to do manual labour when she seemed to be made for something quite different. She replied that there were certain things that she could not have said if she had not done that. The connection between thinking and doing is always with Simone Weil total.

Because of this, she was increasingly desperate at not being able to participate in the war in the way she wanted to. She was finally persuaded that it would be easier to get to England from America and, since her parents were anxious to get both themselves and their daughter there to escape persecution, she accepted in the end to go with them. André and his wife were already there. There were long delays in getting a passage, but in the end they set sail for Casablanca in Morocco on 14 May 1942, and from there reached New York.

New York, London (July 1942–August 1943)

Immediately upon her arrival, Simone was warned that it would not be as easy as she had hoped to get to London. Frustrated and disappointed she set about contacting everyone she knew who had connections with the Free French in London to find an appropriate mission for her. She wrote to the Catholic philosopher Jacques Maritain, to the American Admiral Leahy,

Roosevelt's Chief of Staff who had been Ambassador to Vichy, and wrote also to an English captain who had spoken warmly of France in a radio broadcast previously. Each time she revealed her plan for front-line nurses, and insisted on her need to be where the suffering was greatest. To Maurice Schumann, whom she had known at Henri-IV, she wrote:

> The affliction spread across the surface of the globe obsesses and overwhelms me to the point of annihilating my faculties, and I can only recover them and deliver myself from this obsession if I myself have a large share of danger and suffering. [. . .]
>
> I beg you to obtain for me, if you can, the quantity of suffering and danger necessary to preserve me from being uselessly consumed by grief. I cannot live in the situation in which I find myself at the moment. It leaves me close to despair.[22]

Unable to accomplish what she had come for, she carried on with her writing as best she could, working mainly on the colonial situation. She also spent time in the New York libraries, amassing material for a work on folklore which she wanted to write. Drawn to the life of American Blacks, she frequented Harlem, and was deeply impressed by a service she attended in the Baptist Church there. As anxious as ever to try and clarify her own spiritual position *vis-à-vis* the Church, she made contact with a number of priests, including Father Couturier, to whom she wrote the long *Lettre à un religieux (Letter to a Priest)*, asking precise questions about her own ideas, to try and establish which ones were heretical. One gleam of light was afforded by the birth of Sylvie, her brother's daughter, in whom she took great delight and a keen interest. Given her own position on the threshold of the Church, it is interesting to note that she strongly advised André and his wife to have Sylvie baptised, which they did.

Finally, through the good offices of Maurice Schumann, she heard that André Philip, Secretary of the Interior with the Free French Forces in London, was prepared to bring her to London and give her work. Overjoyed, she left New York on 10 November, arriving at Liverpool around the 25th. André Philip sent her to Louis Closon, head of action in France, who put her to work on reports coming in from committees in the non-occupied zone. It was not at all what she wanted, but she bent herself to the task,

43

and from her pen came an amazing flow of writings, mostly short papers, but including the long essay *L'Enracinement*, which begins with a rethinking of the Declaration of the Rights of Man in terms of obligations, these in turn being defined in relation to one's needs. These writings were not at all understood by her superiors, who wanted her rather to leave aside what they saw as abstract speculation, and talk about practicalities.

One or two of her ideas had perhaps an immediate effect, however. The *Conseil National de la Résistance*, formed a little later, could owe something to the 'Conseil Suprême de la Révolte', which she had proposed in her essay 'Réflexions sur la révolte' (*EL* 109–25), although she was against the idea of a national Council. In 1943, the new Declaration of the Rights of Man, published in the Resistance press, contained a list not only of rights but of duties.

She worked without stopping, often staying in her office all night. Her headaches returned, she ate less and less, consumed by the obsession to be given a dangerous mission in France. Her health deteriorated, although she let no word get back to her parents in America on her true condition. She wrote to them frequently, and her letters talk of London in the springtime, her discovery of English food, the humour and kindness of Londoners, her landlady and her two sons. She continued to put the address of her lodgings right to the end. But on 15 April she collapsed, and was immediately taken to the Middlesex hospital. Tuberculosis was diagnosed, but she was not thought impossible to save. However, she would not, or could not, eat the food necessary for her recovery, and after a short while the initial slight improvement ceased, and her condition remained stationary thereafter. She was very weak, but wanted nevertheless to pursue the question of her relationship with the Church, and had several visits from the Abbé de Naurois, chaplain to the Free French in London. There is an account of some unnamed person, not a priest, baptising her with water from the tap around this time. Details are hard to ascertain, but it would seem that, if the gesture was in fact made, Simone did not attach great importance to it, since she never subsequently asked to partake of the Sacraments, and when she was asked her religion on entering the sanatorium at Ashford, she asked them to put 'none'. In any case, she would have known that such a baptism is valid only if the person concerned is in immediate danger of death, which she was not at that time, nor did she think she was.

She was, however, extremely debilitated, as she tells Closon in her letter of resignation on 26 July: she was 'finished, broken beyond any possibility of repair', although she sees a possibility of surviving perhaps another few years — but only with the help of her parents. Her resignation was provoked, therefore, not essentially by her state of health, but by conditions within the Free French, where disputes and rivalries had broken out, and Simone felt she had no further role to play. In addition, she felt the gap had grown too wide between what she felt her vocation was and what André Philip wanted of her. He had apparently complained to someone one day of not being able to 'use her intelligence'. But her intelligence, which she claims to be totally ordinary, is intrinsically not 'usable': 'Intelligences which are entirely, exclusively abandoned and devoted to the truth are usable by no human being, including the one in which they reside. I don't have the possibility of using my own intelligence; how could I put it at the disposal of Philip?'[23]

By the end of June, she asked to be transferred to a sanatorium. She wanted to see the countryside again, and was aware that the doctors at the hospital felt that she was not cooperating in her own treatment. She was eventually transferred to the sanatorium at Ashford in Kent, on 17 August. She was too weak to be examined properly, but entirely lucid. She attempted at times to eat a little, but failed to respond adequately, and died on 24 August. She was buried in Ashford New Cemetery; at the funeral there were seven people, including her landlady, and other friends. The priest who was supposed to attend missed his train, and did not arrive, so Maurice Schumann read the prayers. The account of her death which appeared in the Ashford *Express* bore the headline 'French professor starves herself to death', reflecting the coroner's report that 'the deceased did kill and slay herself by refusing to eat whilst the balance of her mind was disturbed', whilst the immediate cause of death was given as 'cardiac failure due to myocardial degeneration of the heart muscles due to starvation and pulmonary tuberculosis'.

A full comprehension of her death can only be achieved, if at all, by taking account of her thought. Even then, certain things will inevitably remain mysterious. One or two points can perhaps be made here, however. Although it is true that she seemed to refuse to eat in the hospital, and therefore to be starving herself voluntarily, it is likely that she was physically unable to nourish herself by that time. Eating had always been difficult for her; there were always things which, from childhood, she found physically repulsive and therefore uneatable. Convinced as she was that her vocation was to share the sufferings of her fellow-countrymen, it would have been imposible for her to eat any more by that time, since depriving herself was the only means she had of expressing solidarity. Ironically, had she been given a dangerous mission, she might have lived longer, barring accidents. She had indomitable courage, and a way of disconcerting her attackers which could well have preserved her, as the episode with the Marseilles police shows. Moreover, she says on many occasions that she finds that danger which she is actually undergoing is much easier to cope with than danger at a distance. She died more than anything else of a frustrated vocation, a vocation which involved her in total identification with the world's affliction. As she says in her letter to Joë Bousquet: 'Happy are they for whom affliction, penetrating their flesh, is that of the world itself in their time. They have the possibility and the function of knowing in its truth, of contemplating in its reality the affliction of the world. That is the true redemptive task. [. . .]/ But wretched are they who, having this task, do not accomplish it'.[24] One may indeed speculate on the radically different orientation that her life might have taken had she been able to take up the post in Algeria which she had been offered, and involve herself at first hand in the destiny of the colonies.

There is a revealing passage in the essay 'Réflexions sur les causes de la liberté et de l'oppression sociale' (mentioned above) where she defines freedom as a relationship between thought and action. A truly free man, she says, would be one 'all of whose actions would proceed from a previous judgment regarding the end he has in view, and the following through of the means appropriate to bringing about that end'.[25] Simone Weil had a view of the end that was crystal clear, but she was denied the means of pursuing it.

Notes

1. Simone Weil gives an account of her spiritual development in the long letter to Father Perrin, written in 1942 as she left France for good, and entitled 'Autobiographie spirituelle' in its published form. This letter and others of the same period can be found in the volume *Attente de Dieu*, 2nd edn, Paris: La Colombe, 1950 (tr. by Emma Craufurd as *Waiting on God*, London: Routledge & Kegan Paul, 1951).
2. In fact, as Simone Pétrement points out, these articles appeared in 1930, just after the revolt at Yen Bay and its subsequent repression by France. Simone Weil must therefore have confused the two dates in her mind, thinking of the articles as she visited the exhibition.
3. English version ('Prospects: Are we heading for the proletarian revolution?') available in *Oppression and Liberty*, tr. Arthur F. Wills and John Petrie, London: Routledge & Kegan Paul, 1958, pp. 1–24.
4. *Leçons de Philosophie de Simone Weil (Roanne 1933–1934)* (presented by Anne Reynaud), Paris: Plon, 1959.
5. Simone Pétrement, *La Vie de Simone Weil*, I, pp. 438–9: 'Nous sommes au début d'une période de dictature plus centralisée et plus oppressive que tout ce que nous connaissons dans l'histoire. [. . .] Un beau jour (peut-être le verrons-nous, peut-être pas), tout s'écroulera dans l'anarchie, et on reviendra à des formes presque primitives de la lutte pour la vie'.
6. Ibid., p. 406: 'Dans aucun pays [. . .] les masses travailleuses ne sont plus misérables, plus opprimées, plus avilies qu'en Russie'.
7. English version in *Oppression and Liberty*, pp. 37–124.
8. As she notes in the *Leçons de Philosophie* (p. 181): 'Celui qui écrase ne sent rien, c'est celui qui est écrasé qui sent'. ('The person who crushes others feels nothing, it's the one who is crushed who feels it'.)
9. *AD* 36: 'Ce contact avec le malheur avait tué ma jeunesse. [. . .] Je savais bien qu'il y avait beaucoup de malheur dans le monde, j'en étais obsedée, mais je ne l'avais jamais constaté par un contact prolongé. Etant en usine, [. . .] le malheur des autres est entré dans ma chair et dans mon âme. [. . .] J'ai reçu là pour toujours la marque de l'esclavage. . . .'.
10. English version available in *Formative Writings, 1929–1941*, ed. and tr. Dorothy Tuck McFarland and Wilhelmina Van Ness, Amherst: University of Massachusetts Press, 1987, pp. 151–226.
11. Father Perrin has identified this village as Povoa do Varzini (J.-M. Perrin, *Mon Dialogue avec Simone Weil*, Paris: Nouvelle Cité, 1984, p. 42).
12. *AD* 36–7: 'Mes parents m'avaient emmenée au Portugal, et là je les ai quittés pour aller seule dans un petit village. [. . .] Dans un état physique misérable, je suis entrée dans ce petit village portugais, qui était, hélas, très misérable aussi, seule, le soir, sous la pleine lune, le jour même de la fête patronale. [. . .] Les femmes des pêcheurs

faisaient le tour des barques, en procession, portant des cierges, et chantaient des cantiques certainement très anciens, d'une tristesse déchirante. [...] Là j'ai eu soundain la certitude que le christianisme est par excellence la religion des esclaves, que des esclaves ne peuvent pas ne pas y adhérer, et moi parmi les autres'.

13. English version available in *Seventy Letters*, tr. Richard Rees, London: Oxford University Press, 1965, pp. 26–30.
14. English version available in *Intimations of Christianity*, tr. Elizabeth Chase Geissbühler, London: Routledge & Kegan Paul, 1957.
15. *AD* 37: 'Là, étant seule dans la petite chapelle romane du XIIe siècle de Santa Maria degli Angeli, incomparable merveille de pureté, où saint François a prié bien souvent, quelque chose de plus fort que moi m'a obligée, pour la première fois de ma vie, à me mettre à genoux'.
16. Ibid: 'Il va de soi qu'au cours de ces offices la pensée de la Passion du Christ est entrée en moi une fois pour toutes'.
17. *AD* 38: 'C'est au cours d'une de ces récitations que [ ] le Christ lui-même est descendu et m'a prise'.
18. André Weil maintained, in conversation with me, that she was aware of such writings, since he had mentioned his own reading of them to her. This does not, of course, prove that she had actually read any mystical writings at the time to which she refers.
19. Translated by Mary McCarthy in *Politics*, II, 11, Nov. 45, pp. 321–31 (repr. in *Simone Weil: An Anthology*, ed. Siân Miles, London: Virago Books, 1986, pp. 182–215).
20. English version ('The Great Beast') available in *Selected Essays (1934–43)*, tr. Richard Rees, London: Oxford University Press, 1962, pp. 89–144.
21. *AD* 40–1: 'Parfois les premiers mots déjà arrachent ma pensée à mon corps et la transportent en un lieu hors de l'espace d'où il n'y a ni perspective ni point de vue. L'espace s'ouvre. L'infinité de l'espace ordinaire de la perception est remplacée par une infinité à la deuxième ou quelquefois troisième puissance. En même temps cette infinité d'infinité s'emplit de part en part de silence, un silence qui n'est pas une absence de son, qui est l'objet d'une sensation positive, plus positive que celle d'un son. Les bruits, s'il y en a, ne me parviennent qu'après avoir traversé ce silence./ Parfois aussi, pendant cette récitation ou à d'autres moments, le Christ est présent en personne, mais d'une présence infiniment plus réelle, plus poignante, plus claire et plus pleine d'amour que cette première fois où il m'a prise'.
22. *EL* 199: 'Le malheur répandu sur la surface du globe terrestre m'obsède et m'accable au point d'annuler mes facultés, et je ne puis les récupérer et me délivrer de cette obsession que si j'ai moi-même une large part de danger et de souffrance. [...]/Je vous supplie de me procurer, si vous pouvez, la quantité de souffrance et de danger utiles qui me préservera d'être stérilement consumée par le chagrin.

Je ne peux pas vivre dans la situation où je me trouve en ce moment. Cela me met tout près du désespoir'.
23. Pétrement, *La Vie de Simone Weil*, II, p. 507: 'Les intelligences entièrement, exclusivement abandonnées et vouées à la vérité ne sont utilisables pour aucun être humain, y compris celui dans lequel elles résident. Je n'ai pas la possibilité d'utiliser ma propre intelligence; comment pourrais-je la mettre à la disposition de Philip?'
24. *PSO* 76: 'Heureux ceux pour qui le malheur entré dans la chair est le malheur du monde lui-même à leur époque. Ceux-là ont la possibilité et la fonction de connaître dans sa vérité, de contempler dans sa réalité le malheur du monde. C'est là la fonction rédemptrice elle-même.[. . .]/Mais infortunés ceux qui ayant cette fonction ne l'accomplissent pas'.
25. *OL* 115: '[Serait tout à fait libre un homme] dont toutes les actions procéderaient d'un jugement préalable concernant la fin qu'il se propose et l'enchaînement des moyens propres à amener cette fin'.

Part II The Works

1 The Good and the Necessary

Simone Weil was first and foremost a philosopher. She was a philosopher, however, who believed in the indissoluble unity of ideas and action, who was convinced that ideas to be valid had to be 'tested' in matter, while remaining faithful to the end of her life to the discipline in which she had been trained and which, as we have seen, she taught for a few brief years. The things of the mind were of supreme value to her, and the right use of the mind she considered the first duty of every human being. Philosophy was thus a matter of vital importance for everyone, because she believed that any human being, no matter how mediocre his or her natural gifts, could and should grasp the central truths of philosophy: what allowed access to the region of truth was not intellectual brilliance but the right quality of attention. A great deal of the effort of her mature years was spent in a meditation on the ways and means of transforming society so that everyone could exercise their intelligence in the lucid grasp of the world around them, instead of being subject to forces beyond their control.

This being so, it is appropriate to start an assessment of the nature and scope of Simone Weil's contribution to our times by a consideration of some of the ideas that form the basis to her thought. While some of them may seem highly abstract in nature, the effort of attention required to grasp them will be amply rewarded by a deeper understanding of Simone Weil's thinking on more precise and concrete problems, as well as of the significance of her life.

The opening section of one of the papers Simone Weil wrote for the Free French in London[1] is entitled 'Profession de foi' ('Profession of faith'), and in it she states the basic premises upon which her thinking was based in those last months before her death and consequently, the foundations of her political and religious philosophy. The essay opens: 'There is a reality situated outside the world, that is to say, outside space and time, outside man's mental universe, outside the whole realm accessible to human faculties./ To this reality corresponds in the centre of man's heart that demand for absolute good which constantly inhabits it, and which finds no object in this world'.[2]

Simone Weil thus posits from the outset a supernatural reality beyond man's immediate apprehension, to which corresponds his desire for good. The belief that this desire for good exists was a fundamental tenet of Simone Weil's philosophy, and appears in a different formulation in other essays and notes, particularly in the later writings. In another of the 'London essays', for instance, she defines the sacred element in every human being, from the cradle to the grave, as 'something which, in spite of all the experience of crimes committed, suffered from and witnessed, expects that good and not evil will be done to him'.[3] This desire for good not only forms a link with a transcendent reality, it is also the only foundation for the respect that a human being should show towards every other creature without exception. Human beings are naturally unequal in their capacities, as in the degree of attention which they command in their fellow-beings at any given moment, and the only foundation for absolute equality of respect is something shared equally by all of them, namely, this desire for good.

The metaphysical foundation of Simone Weil's thought forms in this way a total and harmonious whole with her ethics: to perceive the structure of the universe is at the same time to understand how to treat one's fellow-beings. This identity of perception and ethic is made all the clearer by her insistence in the 'Profession de foi' on the intimate relationship between absolute good and its manifestation in the natural world: all the beauty, justice, order, and obligation experienced in society have their origin in this absolute. She thus implies that the natural world is in some way a stranger to absolute good and its manifestations, that goodness has come from elsewhere, and represents 'another reality'. What Simone Weil meant by this 'other reality' involves, however, complex and often abstract ideas with which modern readers are not generally familiar, and it is perhaps useful at this point to indicate some of the sources for her ideas, as well as showing the personal way in which she developed them.

The main source is, of course, Plato, to whom Simone Weil was introduced as a student, particularly by Alain. She never lost her love of Plato; many of her ideas and formulations have a Platonic ring, and she is indeed one of the very few twentieth-century Platonists, which is why her vocabulary can sometimes seem strange to our ears. Plato's whole philosophy, according to her, was founded on the idea of absolute good, and his fundamental perception was of the distance between the good and the necessary, those two elements which are at the root of the contradictions we experience in our very existence: 'The essential contradiction of the human condition is that man is subject to force and desires justice. He is subject to necessity and desires good'.[4] She retains this Platonic terminology to the end of her life, though it is clear that, increasingly, by the 'good' she means God. The reason she keeps Plato's term is probably partly the great discretion she maintained regarding her own religious experience, partly the desire to retain the impersonal element which can be lacking in the traditional Judæo-Christian idea of God, and which she found so important, because it underlined precisely the crucial perception of the transcendence of God, of the 'other reality'.

Given that this reality is so utterly 'other', what can be said about it that is intelligible? Simone Weil herself claimed to have refused prior to her mystical experiences to consider the problem of God, believing that we lack the data to come to a proper conclusion and that therefore the best way of not making a mistake was to leave the question aside: being in the world, our affair was to adopt the best attitude towards its problems and not concern ourselves with what was beyond our comprehension (*AD* 32). Probably partly for this reason, when she talks about 'the good', it is very often in terms of a relationship, a contradiction between what man desires and what he is in fact subjected to, as in the passage quoted above, or in the form of myths illustrating one aspect or another of the relationship between the good and the necessary.

Perhaps one of these myths is therefore an appropriate place to begin. One of the most revealing, as well as one of the most fundamental, is her account of the creation of the universe, which differs radically from the traditional account given in Genesis. Firstly, to the Judæo-Christian idea of a creation *ex nihilo* she prefers the Platonic concept of creation being an organisation by God of pre-existent matter (*IP* 29). Necessity, that network of relationships permeating the world of matter, is something God had to take account of when creating, a feature which limited His design. In this way, God could be said to submit to necessity (*PSO* 35). A further characteristic of her myth is that creation is an act not of expansion but of retreat or diminution on God's part. God before creation was more perfect than God having created, since before the creative act He was totally self-sufficient. The independent self-contemplation of the Creator is destroyed by the coming into existence of another being, creation, and the resulting diminution of God is the cause of His suffering. The suffering of Christ on the Cross is hence only a reflection of the primordial suffering occasioned by the birth of the universe, and the same conflict is experienced by man as the contradiction between what he desires and what he is, between his aspirations to goodness and his submission to necessity.

The myth which Simone Weil finds in Plato and develops thus is clearly very rich in its implications, and it is worth considering now some of these. First of all, if creation is an act of retreat on God's part, it would seem that His omnipotence is in some way limited. It is true that Simone Weil, seeing power in general as a base attribute belonging to the sphere of necessity rather than that of good, does not emphasise the power of God. But she nevertheless wants to retain the sense of wholeness that such power implies, so concludes that God is omnipotent in so far as His retreat is voluntary (*CS* 67): the true God is one who is all-powerful, but who refuses to command everywhere He has the power to do so (*AD* 105). In this way she avoids partially, but not totally, the age-old and insoluble problem of the existence of evil in a world created by a good and all-powerful God. If God is at the same time omnipotent and loving, why does He not prevent evil? The idea of the retreat of God attenuates the difficulty, as does her notion that we must think of God as being at an infinite distance in order to preserve His innocence (*C2* 148). Goodness is God's essential attribute, as far as Simone Weil is concerned: all the rest is secondary (*PSO* 47). In fact, it is not for her an attribute at all, in the sense that God's being could be separated from His goodness: His mode of being is goodness.

Given the supremacy of goodness in Simone Weil's conception of God, it is not surprising that we find her suggesting that in a certain sense the question of His existence is not important. Existence and goodness are not in any case commensurate: earthly things exist, but they are not absolute good. Whether absolute good exists or not, there is no other absolute good (*CS* 284). All that is required of man is that he should abandon relative, earthly good and direct his attention towards the absolute, its existence or otherwise being a matter of indifference. In fact, Simone Weil claims that desire for absolute good is the same as possessing it, that in the region of the supernatural, desire is productive of being. 'It is in the case of false good that desire and possession are different; for true good there is no difference.'[5] She notes with obvious approval the Nordic creation-myth, where in the primeval darkness the crow desired light, and light was created. The question of the existence of absolute good as object of desire is thus clearly on a different plane from that of earthly phenomena, and denial of the 'existence' of absolute good becomes more than an intellectual game. If one reflects at the same time on her mystical experiences, which are proof if any were needed of the reality of the supernatural, one perceives a profound tendency at work in Simone Weil's thought in general. Like many mystics, she frequently prefers to express knowledge of God in negative terms: 'we can know only one thing about God: that he is what we are not'.[6] We should cultivate a 'negative faith', in terms of which 'nothing that we can grasp is God' (*C2* 108). She clearly appreciated the tendency in some oriental philosophy, in particular Taoism, to express God in terms of the impersonal, 'the Way', opposing this to the Western inclination to emphasise the personal, anthropomorphised aspect.

She in fact goes further when she suggests a technique for purifying the concept of God by denying His very existence, what she calls 'purifying atheism' ('l'athéisme purificateur') (*C1* 257). This is not simply the claim I already referred to above, that the order of goodness is superior to that of being, but a way of ridding our notion of God of all anthropomorphic elements. We should thus at times pray to God while simultaneously thinking that He does not exist.

Simone Weil's emphasis on the non-existence, hypothetical or not, of God, and yet of His supreme reality as goodness, presents problems only when viewed from the limited perspective of a certain traditional Judæo-Christian theology. In other traditions, existence is often seen as a limitation, because of its necessary association with the specific — if something exists, it does so distinct from other beings, and derives its existence from its limits — and mystical experience in Christianity and elsewhere has frequently adopted a negative approach to the idea of

57

God. Experience of the Divine through personal contact has often been associated with a desire to emphasise the utter otherness of the Supreme Being — as Simone Weil would say, the gulf between the good and the necessary. In any case, for her, the experience was the ultimate criterion: as she remarks, faced with two people who have no experience of God, the one who denies His existence is probably closer to the truth.

Simone Weil's approach to the concept of God therefore emphasises both His transcendence and the possibility of a real and personal contact. What does she have to say regarding the other pole of the Platonic good–necessity duality? The very fact that she sees God as Creator, as imposing order on matter, implies an intimate contact between the two, and indeed some of the images she uses to describe the act of creation suggest contact to the point of identity. God in creation 'becomes necessity' (*C*2 67), creation 'bears God's signature'(*C*3 308). It is in any case willed by God, and entirely obedient to His purpose. As far as man is concerned, necessity is the structure of intelligible reality itself, a network of relationships at work in matter, which allow the human mind to grasp reality. Simone Weil emphasises the essential relationship between necessity and reality: everything that is real is subject to necessity, and it is this fact which allows us to distinguish between the real and the imaginary (*C*2 170) — bearing in mind that for Simone Weil the imaginary is that which has no authentic existence. Necessity is in fact a 'criterion of the real', in the sense that whatever is not subject to necessary relationships, the real existence of other phenomena, has no reality. It is true, she says, that in one sense also there is identity between the good and the real: but the resulting contradiction is almost a guarantee of the truth of the proposition. It is only in the sphere of the imaginary that thought does not meet any contradiction: the imagination leaps over obstacles and recreates reality according to its own desires (*C*2 239). Necessity, by contrast, is the world of the mathematician, 'thought in action' (*IP* 154; *C*3 141, 143, 144). Phenomena subject to necessity are governed by the existence of other phenomena, in other words limits, unlike the world of the imagination, which knows no boundaries. Everything is possible to the imagination.

The idea of limits plays an important part in Simone Weil's thinking, not only in her description of the physical world but also in the moral lessons which she draws from it. It is important to note, however, that the notion of limits is not for her first and foremost a moral one; it is not a question of man's moral responsibility not to overstep certain limits. Simone Weil's conception of limits is much closer to the Greek nemesis, where excess brings about a natural restoration of balance. Nemesis is 'a sanction of geometric rigour, which automatically punishes the abuse of force' (*SG* 22), a simple mechanical process as valid in the lives of human beings as it is in the world of matter. Simone Weil's disinclination to oppose Hitler before Munich was based at least in part on the belief that his power was limited by its own abuse, and that the Nazi regime could turn out to be of very limited duration. In the world of relationships between individuals, man is subject to the same inescapable forces: when, for instance, two parties to a disagreement are equal in strength, a sort of natural justice operates, and a discussion takes place. When one party is stronger, there is no discussion possible: the weaker simply accepts what the stronger imposes (*IP* 136). The stronger has then the illusion of omnipotence, not realising that his power is limited in exactly the same way as all other phenomena, because force hypnotises, plunges those who wield it into a dream-world (*C*1 141). Force is, of course, not necessity, rather an aspect of necessity, the way in which man experiences necessity in his contact with others and in his struggle for existence.

It is largely the experience of necessary relationships as force that teaches us the gulf between necessity and the good, in Simone Weil's view. In a world subject to force it is not difficult to see goodness as absent. It is also tempting, she says, to attenuate that gulf by imposing a providential pattern upon events. Simone Weil was bitterly critical of what she considered to be the Roman concept of Providence, and which she describes as 'a personal intervention of God in the universe to adjust certain means with a view to particular ends'.[7] For her, such an intervention was as absurd as it was blasphemous. Why, for instance, should I attribute to Providence the fact that lightning strikes a centimetre away from me without touching me, but fail to see the same hand at work when the lightning strikes a kilometre away? From our limited perspective, we see only those relationships that concern us directly, and ignore the others. In truth, we should see Providence in every event without exception, in that all events are willed by God. 'Divine Providence is not [. . .] an anomaly in the order of the world. It is the order of the world itself.'[8] Hence, to take a concrete historical example, it is wrong to see divine inspiration in the actions of Joan of Arc. Like other combatants through the ages she was simply subject to the blind mechanical forces which govern the universe.

A true perspective on force is something quite other, according to Simone Weil, and its illustration can be seen admirably in the Greek epic poem, the *Iliad*. The essay which Simone Weil wrote on it while in Marseilles during the war, *'L'Iliade ou le poème de la force'* (mentioned in Part I above), is a remarkable piece of interpretation, quite different in its inspiration from traditional interpretations, and centring around the idea of force. It is clear that she was inspired directly by the war-situation in which she found herself, and wished the essay to be interpreted as a comment on both the general and the particular. According to her reading, the *Iliad* is a truly faithful account of the submission of man to force, and a lucid and compassionate statement of the non-intervention of the Divine in the affairs of men. The real hero of the *Iliad*, she says, is force, that force which turns men into inanimate objects. Sometimes it kills, sometimes death is delayed, but always it turns a man to stone (*SG* 12–13), and the person wielding force behaves exactly as if he were confronted with an inanimate object (*SG* 15). She gives the illustration of a master and his slave: there is no difference, she says, between throwing a stone to chase away a dog, and telling a slave to get rid of it (*AD* 104).

The particular genius of the *Iliad*, however, is to have portrayed the protagonists not as masters and slaves, conquerors and conquered, but as all being equally subject to force. No one possesses force in the end, even those who have the illusion of doing so. All are caught up in a mechanism which has its own absurd momentum, so that war becomes an end in itself, and no one any longer understands why it is being pursued. A mythical entity takes the place of the original cause, so that people can believe that all the sacrifices demanded by the war have not been in vain. Simone Weil thus underlines the unreality of war, and in this way, although she was by this time totally committed to the struggle against Hitler, she prolongs her earlier pacifist thinking, when she was convinced of the nonsense of fighting for some apparent slight to the prestige of France, when such an engagement would have lost for the workers the real improvements they had gained in their condition in the struggles of the mid-1930s. She brings home this same truth in another essay of her pacifist period, 'Ne recommençons pas la guerre de Troie' ('Words and War') (*EH* 256–72),[9] where she again evokes the Trojan War, pointing out that with the exception of Paris, no one in either the Greek or the Trojan camp was in the slightest degree interested in Helen. 'Our political universe', she claims, 'is peopled entirely with myths and monsters; we recognise only entities and absolutes.'[10] Our political vocabulary abounds in words like nation, security, capitalism, Communism, each of which is supposed to represent an absolute, and be treated as such, independent of the particular political circumstances. It is of such stuff that wars have always been made.

Such reflections, with their pessimism and their lack of partisanship, were not calculated to please those whose political ideas or ambitions depended on mystification. Simone Weil's view of force governing conquerers and conquered alike leads logically to a dispassionate and compassionate assessment of the participants, one which she claimed to find in the *Iliad*. Because of the very even-handedness of some of her remarks on the combatants in the Second World War, her views were often misunderstood: her inability to hate the Germans because of the crimes of their leaders, her desire (for instance in the long essay on the origins of Hitlerism, mentioned in Part I above) to understand the historical processes which had made Hitler possible, and furthermore, her discovery of the same cultural tendencies within the French nation, were severely criticised by those who felt that an enemy was an enemy, and that to try to understand was half-way to condoning.

For Simone Weil, however, it was the first duty of every human being to understand the forces at work in the universe, and man's place in it, because a right understanding of that place was the only source of right action. From Plato again she derived inspiration for that understanding, in particular from his mythical account of humanity chained up in a cave, able to see only the reflections of objects thrown by the light of a fire behind them, and never the objects themselves. Such is our condition, says Simone Weil: we see only shadows, which we take for real objects, and we live and die in an absence of truth. Such an interpretation has profound implications for the world of action: if we can never be certain of being 'in the truth', we should treat all solutions to problems, particularly in the field of politics, as provisional. The idea of a Utopia is positively dangerous since, although from time to time and by chance our ideas will contain an element of truth, most of the time they will simply conform to the workings of necessity. Man's natural condition is darkness, and he should beware of acting as though he were in broad daylight.

Such an assessment is clearly at the heart of the development of Simone Weil's political thinking, with her growing scepticism regarding political action, and her progressive refusal of revolutionary activity in, for instance, the syndicalist movement. Her political pessimism made her appreciate the thought of the Renaissance political philosopher, Machiavelli, whom she saw as developing Plato's ideas on the fundamentally evil nature of society. Society was 'an irreducible evil which one can only try to limit' (SG 91), and 'the reform or the transformation of society can have no reasonable object other than to render it the least evil possible'.[11] To do this, a dispassionate analysis of the mechanism of social relationships is required: necessity being the raw material of society, sociology should be the scientific analysis of necessity. Machiavelli, whom Simone Weil sees as a pioneer sociologist, had the great merit of having begun this analysis. Marx continued the same work: although Simone Weil was deeply critical of Marx in many respects, and considered many of his conclusions to have been erroneous, he nevertheless pursued the same essential goal as Machiavelli in his attempt to discover the workings of society, and the nature of the forces that oppress human beings. Marx's analysis of oppression, which is after all only composed of relationships of force, particularly impressed Simone Weil: he understood, for example, that the State, by simple virtue of its nature, would continue to oppress as long as it existed, whoever held the reins of power. Marx's observations on the enslavement of working people to the process of production finds an echo in Simone Weil's analysis of her factory experience where, as we have seen, her sense of enslavement was paramount. She goes far beyond Marx, however, in her perception of the forces that enslave man at work in the universe in general. It is noteworthy how frequently the concept of slavery is used in the essay on the *Iliad*: force enslaves both those that wield it and those that submit to it, and the process is no different in its essence from what goes on in the factory. Man has only freed himself from the tyranny of nature in order to enslave himself to his fellow-beings, as she says in the essay 'Réflexions sur les causes de la liberté et de l'oppression sociale' (referred to in Part I above). Furthermore, it is a process to which there is no end, in her view: from time immemorial, oppression has been considered as a simple usurpation, and the remedy seen as the abolition of the oppressors. But the immediate installation of a new tyranny after the destruction of the old at the time of the French Revolution was only the most glaring example of a permanent phenomenon: relationships of force change, those that wielded force become those that submit to it, but the relationships remain (*OL* 80–81). Slavery in one form or another would seem to be a permanent feature of the human condition.

This would seem a very bleak assessment of man's place in the universe, particularly as regards his capacity for positive action. If the good to which he aspires remains beyond his grasp, if he is permanently subject to an indifferent necessity which exposes him to relationships of force which frequently brutalise and maim him, when it is not he himself doing the brutalising and maiming, and if, finally, he exists in a condition of permanent mental darkness and illusion, so that he can never be sure of having assessed correctly the situation in which he finds himself, what hope is there for taking action to improve his lot and that of his fellows? This is a permanent dilemma for Simone Weil, and one to which she was acutely sensitive. When war broke out and conflict became inevitable, her first thought, as we have seen, was to participate, even though this meant a rejection of her previous pacifist ideas. In many ways this was the cruellest dilemma of all those with which she was faced: although, for example, in the field of industrial work she had become disillusioned with the prospects of collective action to effect change, she was able to continue to elaborate ideas which she believed would lessen the enslavement of the worker to his conditions of work. In the war situation, however, she was participating voluntarily in something she saw as a total evil, and from which no good could conceivably come. How could one reconcile oneself to act at all in such circumstances?

Simone Weil found a partial solution to the problem in her reading of the *Bhagavad Gītā*, the Sanskrit poem which she discovered in the early months of the war, and which deeply impressed her. She immediately sensed the relevance of this account of a society caught up in a war situation, and her notebooks of the period bear many references to the central characters. At the beginning of the poem, the hero, Arjuna, is faced with a situation of civil war in which he is obliged to take up arms against his own family. His natural revulsion to do this, and the progressive revelation by Krishna of the limitations of such an attitude, form the subject of the poem. In Simone Weil's interpretation, Arjuna hesitates to take part in an action in which he can see no good, and wants to be convinced that he is fighting for a just cause. Krishna, however, reveals to him progressively that in a world governed by necessity there is no such thing as a truly just cause, no absolute good or evil, and that to a certain extent one has to accept being a mere passage for the workings of necessity. One must 'allow necessity to work within oneself' (*C*2 154), 'accept submission to necessity and act only through wielding it' (*C*1 150). This kind of activity is essentially passive, consisting in a resolve to restrict oneself to immediate acts which one cannot avoid, rather than trying to see a long-term good in a particular action. It is a kind of spiritual immobility, the simple accomplishment of prescribed acts, neither more nor less. No merit attaches to such acts of obedience: it is at one and the same time the maximum and the minimum possible. Simone Weil calls it 'l'action non-agissante' ('non-acting action' or 'passive action'), which she defines as 'doing only what one cannot not do' (*C*1 222). It is in this sense that Arjuna is persuaded in the end to fight, not because he has any desire for victory, but because he realises that he has no choice: 'He would prefer not to fight and wallows in his feelings of pity. But if he asks himself clearly: "is it possible for me not to fight?" he cannot, at that moment, in that situation, answer yes'.[12] The relevance of this reflection to Simone Weil's own situation is obvious: in the early months of the war, stunned and humiliated by the events that had overtaken her country, and yet still perceiving war as an overwhelming catastrophe, she needed to find a justification for action. She knew that she would not be fighting for any absolute ideal, that she would be contributing to the suffering and misery that war brought in its train — but when she asked herself 'is it possible for me not to fight?' she knew she could not answer yes. It was, literally, 'the least she could do'. There is therefore in her response to the situation no feeling that she was 'doing good': such a concept was alien to her pessimism in the social sphere, and to her conviction that goodness, as an absolute, was elsewhere. In another note which also dates from the war years, she attempts to define a 'good action', and her definition is remarkable by its clear-headed use of paradox: 'An action is good if one can perform it while keeping one's attention and intention fixed on pure and impossible goodness, without obscuring by lies either the desirability or the impossibility of pure goodness'.[13] The sphere of necessity in which we operate is what she calls the region of good and evil, where the good is frequently hardly any better than the opposing evil. What is possible is not good, and what is good is not possible.

Such, then, are some of the implications in the practical and political sphere of Simone Weil's basic metaphysical vision. It is a vision characterised by a conviction of the reality of absolutes, but also by a great wariness as to their application in the real world. Uncompromising in its desire for truth, her vision is also a warning that in a certain sense the truth is beyond our grasp, and that we never truly 'know' anything at all. Such a vision, while earning her the condemnation of those whose revolutionary politics found her pessimism unacceptable, is perhaps, because of its recognition of the limits of human endeavour, the only basis for a truly compassionate attitude towards one's fellow-beings.

Notes

1. 'Etude pour une déclaration des obligations envers l'être humain' ('Study for a declaration of obligations towards the human being'), *EL* 74–84, English version available in *Selected Essays (1934–43)* tr. Richard Rees, London: Oxford University Press, 1965, pp. 219–27.
2. *EL* 74: 'Il est une réalité située hors du monde, c'est-à-dire hors de l'espace et du temps, hors de l'univers mental de l'homme, hors de tout le domaine que les facultés humaines peuvent atteindre./A cette réalité répond au centre du cœur de l'homme cette exigence d'un

bien absolu qui y habite toujours et ne trouve jamais aucun objet en ce monde'.
3. *EL* 13: '[Il y a depuis la petite enfance jusqu'à la tombe, au fond du cur de tout être humain,] quelque chose qui, malgré toute l'expérience des crimes commis, soufferts et observé, s'attend invinciblement à ce qu'on lui fasse de bien et non du mal'.
4. *OL* 209: 'La contradiction essentielle de la condition humaine, c'est que l'homme est soumis à la force, et désire la justice. Il est soumis à la nécessité et désire le bien'.
5. *CS* 110: 'C'est pour les faux biens que désir et possession sont différents; pour le vrai bien, il n'y a aucune différence'.
6. *C*2 127: 'Nous ne pouvons savoir qu' une chose de Dieu: qu'il est ce que nous ne sommes pas'.
7. *E* 236 '[La conception de la Providence qui répond au Dieu du type romain,] c'est une intervention personnelle de Dieu dans l'univers pour adjuster certains moyens en vue de fins particulières'.
8. *E* 241: 'La Providence divine n'est pas [. . .] une anomalie dans l'ordre du monde. C'est l'ordre du monde lui-même'.
9. English version ('Words and War') by Bowden Broadwater available in *Politics*, III, 3, Mar. 46, pp. 69–73.
10. *EH* 259: 'Notre univers politique est exclusivement peuplé de mythes et de monstres; nous n'y connaissons que des entités, que des absolus'.
11. *SG* 90: 'La réforme ou la transformation de la société ne peut pas avoir d'autre objet raisonnable que de la rendre la moins mauvaise possible'.
12. *C*1 222: 'Il voudrait ne pas combattre et se perd dans son émotion de pitié. Mais s'il se demande clairement: "est-ce que je peux ne pas combattre?" il ne peut pas, à ce moment, dans cette situation, répondre oui'.
13. *C*3 30: 'Est bonne l'action qu'on peut accomplir en maintenant l'attention et l'intention totalement orientées vers le bien pur et impossible, sans voiler par aucun mensonge ni la désirabilité ni l'impossibilité du bien pur'.

2 The Great Beast

The fact that Simone Weil was so acutely aware of the problems of right action in a world governed by mechanical forces, and her conviction that absolute goodness was a reality of a totally different order from anything realisable in everyday acts, made her extraordinarily sensitive to attempts, which she found not only in the contemporary reality around her, but throughout history, to confuse the orders of goodness and necessity. This sensitivity colours and conditions her whole approach to history, and it is no exaggeration to say that her judgements on society and historical events in the end always stem from whether or not the collectivity concerned was able to retain the sense of the distance between the good and the necessary.

If the judgement is frequently negative, it is a result, in Simone Weil's view, of the nature of the collectivity itself. For her it was a source of evil far more powerful than that of the individual ego. As I shall show later, the ego, with its natural tendency to interpret everything as a function of its own desires and ambitions, is a factor for wrong-doing, but society itself, the collectivity, is much more dangerous. When Simone Weil talks about the Devil, it is nearly always in relation to social rather than carnal temptations; for example, she quotes as Christ's supreme temptation the offer made by the Devil of all the kingdoms of the earth. The prestige of the collectivity, and the way it conditions the thought of the individual, is well-nigh irresistible, so much so that, according to Simone Weil, most of the time we do not even realise that we are thinking or acting merely under social pressure. The collectivity seems in some way to be transcendent to the individual, and becomes in this way an end in itself, a sort of false divinity to which the individual is entirely subject.

This divinisation of the collectivity is what Simone Weil called idolatry, which is clearly different from what is normally meant by that term. For her, idolatry is almost always social in its nature, although it forms the essential element in her criticism of aspects of certain religious traditions, notably those of Judaism and the Catholic Church. She is almost casual in her approach to what is traditionally looked on as idolatry. Monotheism does not protect against idolatry: 'To know the Deity only as power and not as goodness, is idolatry, and it matters little then whether there is one God or several'.[1] Polytheism does not bother her: she considers the representation in the *Iliad* of the Olympic pantheon to be designed as a comic interlude, and estimates Plato's knowledge of God as supreme goodness to be of far greater significance. She even admits the necessity of idols for man in his earthly state, but cautions that they should be the least harmful possible (*CS* 113). Idols in the literal sense of images she considers almost a protection against more serious ones, since 'you can't stand in front of a lump of sculptured wood and say "You have made heaven and earth" '.[2]

'More serious' ones are always those that deny the gulf between goodness and necessity. Idols, she claims, are instances of relative good conceived as good outside any relationship, or earthly objects in which absolute good is falsely incarnated. What should be a means becomes an end, taking on an absolute value, and this reversal of relationships accounts, in Simone Weil's view, for 'all that is insane and blood-stained throughout history' (*OL* 95). This observation is at the basis of her criticism of Marx who, according to her, idolised the notions of progress and history. From her student days onwards, she was deeply suspicious of the idea of progress, claiming that in the moral sphere it had no meaning. Human existence was characterised by fluctuations between relative good and evil, and Marx's claim that these fluctuations could somehow produce absolute good by, for instance, putting power in the hands of the proletariat who would then bring about justice on earth, had the unreality of a dream. The march of history could only produce variations on the basic relationships between various power-groups. As we have already seen, if the oppressed are ready to take power, it is because they already possess a force superior to that of the oppressor. One of Marx's fundamental contradictions was to believe on the one hand that force governs human relationships, and on the other to retain Hegel's idea of history as the progress of Spirit through the universe, so that matter contains within itself the basis of its own perfectibility. But how can we imagine that a society governed by relationships of production could ever become a classless society? How can matter produce Utopia, she asks:

Marx claimed to have 'set straight' the Hegelian dialectic which he accused of being 'upside down'; he substituted matter for spirit as the motive force in history; but by an extraordinary paradox, he conceived history, on the basis of that correction, as if he attributed to matter what is the very essence of spirit, namely an aspiration towards the good.[3]

Marx was thus an idolater, whose idol was the society of the future; but since every idolater needs an object here and now, he made an idol of that part of society which was about to operate the transformation, in other words, the proletariat (*OL* 210). Their actions were then judged not relative to an absolute good, but relative to the final end which for Marx had taken its place, so that the age of justice and virtue which was the aim of society became also its judge. In this way, anything which could hasten the promised end was good, not in itself, but in relation to the future just society.

This appraisal is what Simone Weil calls 'group morality', which forbids critical assessment and which, because it is literally 'beyond good and evil', is considered to be justice itself. Relating it to other forms of 'idolatry', she further defines it as the phenomenon of 'setting aside': in other words, the relationships between things which normally convey relative status on them are suppressed. It is a phenomenon particularly associated with the collective, with the kind of patriotism that one has towards a country, or a party, or a Church. 'Everything that is covered with the prestige of the collective is set aside and removed from certain relationships.'[4]

Marx was not the first to believe in the perfectibility of society through history, according to Simone Weil, although it is an idea we associate particularly with the nineteenth century. She takes the idea back to the origins of Christianity in Judaism, and to the notion of 'divine education', with its associated concept of spiritual evolution, which has been used throughout the ages to explain, or explain away, crimes committed in the name of religion. While 'the great mistake of the Marxists and of the whole nineteenth century was to believe that by walking straight ahead you go up in the air',[5] it is a mistake that can be traced right back to the Judæo-Christian notion of history as 'directed continuity' (*C3* 306), in other words, that history has a purpose and a fulfilment in precise events which betoken or lead to improvement in man.

The concept of idolatry as the worship of history is thus at the root of Simone Weil's criticism of Judaism and of certain aspects of Christianity. At the heart of Judaism and of the Christian notion of revelation is the idea of time as becoming, as development, as progress, and this is in direct contrast with Greek thought which tends often to interpret history as a cyclic motion. The idea of history as progress revealing the will of God, and its corollary, the notion of a chosen people who serve as the instrument of that will, was profoundly antipathetical to Simone Weil. She refused totally the idea of the Old Testament being the progressive revelation of the God of Israel as universal God, seeing only the political consequences of election; a God who 'chooses' a particular people cannot at the same time manifest the impartiality which, for her, is the characteristic of the true God. The God who operates through history and modifies nature for his own ends could not be the one who in creating the universe submitted Himself to necessity. God does not intervene in human affairs, so that 'the very notion of a chosen people is incompatible with the knowledge of the true God'.[6] Since the promises made to Israel by Jehovah applied to the temporal domain, being promises concerning Israel's destiny, Simone Weil accuses him of being a temporal and terrestrial God, and considers Moses to have been a politician rather than a spiritual leader. Moses was above all the founder of a State, who 'wanted to appear as the envoy of a powerful God who makes temporal promises'.[7]

When she says that Moses conceived of religion 'as a simple instrument of national grandeur', it is obvious that she is leaving on one side the spiritual element in the commandments given to Israel, with their profound ethical consequences. It was the nationalism of Israel which was most significant in her eyes, however, and was responsible for the idolatry which she saw in that nation. Idols being forbidden, Israel became a replacement for a statue of Jehovah. Israel is for her 'an attempt at supernatural social life ... revelation translated into social terms' (*C*3 106), in other words, an attempt at incarnating the absolute in the relative, without passing through a mediating term. The idea of mediation was of great importance to Simone Weil, and one to which I will return in Chapter 6. The refusal of mediation, in her eyes, resulted frequently in this confusion of what should remain distinct, the absolute and the relative, the good and the necessary. The direct approach to God by man in Judaism is one of that religion's fundamental characteristics, and the resulting moral presence of God in man at every level of his life is one of its most positive aspects. For Simone Weil, however, this very characteristic was its limitation, and the reason why it had chosen to confuse the temporal and the eternal: having refused the idea of mediation which it found in surrounding civilisations, Israel tried to use the nation itself as a way towards God. In her view, the only contact possible between God and man was through the person of a mediator: apart from this, the only possible presence of God is collective and national. Israel at one and the same moment chose a national God and refused the idea of a mediator. The result was that, although there was a movement at times towards true monotheism, Israel always fell back into its conception of the Divinity as a tribal God (*C*3 255).

One of the most unfortunate consequences of this 'idolatry', and of the intervention of God in human affairs in general was, in Simone Weil's view, a confusion between prosperity and virtue. The logic of a statement such as 'And the Lord was with Joseph, and he prospered' (Genesis 39.2) was clearly repugnant to her. It is a fact that in much of the Old Testament the equivalence is made between doing right in God's eyes and material prosperity. Even in the Psalms, where there is frequently a profoundly personal sense of sin as evil in itself, rather than simply an act bringing down punishment on its perpetrator, all too often repentance is followed by God's promise to give Israel victory over her enemies. Even when God's mercy prevails, the idea that God, being just, has the right to reward and punish according to merit is seldom lost sight of. The general sense is that when Israel does right in the eyes of the Lord, the nation prospers; when it disobeys God's commandments, then Israel suffers misfortune, battles are lost and the enemy triumphs. The reverse side of this proposition, that a beaten enemy is guilty simply because beaten, is totally unacceptable to Simone Weil: 'The Hebrews saw in misfortune the sign of sin and consequently a legitimate reason for contempt; they saw their beaten enemies as being rejected by God himself and condemned to expiate their crimes, a view which made cruelty permissible and even indispensable'.[8]

It is necessary I believe to underline this aspect of Simone

Weil's criticism of Judaism, because it lies at the heart of her rejection of her ethnic background. This rejection has often been misunderstood, and frequently condemned, and there are indeed features of it that perplex. Her criticisms were, to say the least, untimely, since she continued to express them when the persecutions of Jews from which she herself suffered, in the years leading up to the war and, more particularly, during the war itself, were well under way, although it is unlikely that she knew the full horror of what was going on. In mitigation it must be said that none of her pronouncements are anti-Semitic in a vulgar sense and although she did not single out Jews for special attention during the considerable period when she was assisting refugees from Germany and elsewhere, it is clear that she gave help to Jews and non-Jews alike in her Resistance work in Marseilles. In London, in 1943, it seems she still had not grasped the scope of the Nazi persecution of the Jews: in a paper on the legitimacy of the Provisional Goverment, she writes of the lack of accountability of political leaders under the Third Republic; even when crimes were committed by these men, the penalties were derisory, so that if they had wished to promulgate a law condemning to death all Jewish people without distinction, the only penalty for so horrific a crime would have been their loss of power through the ballot box (*EL* 68). She could hardly have written in this vein if she had realised how closely this hypothetical situation reflected what was actually going on.

On her approach to the Jewish tradition, she has been much reproached for her ignorance of texts other than the Old Testament, and it is true that she lacked both breadth and depth in some aspects of the tradition: she can hardly be reproached for an imperfect knowledge of a civilisation with which she felt she had no affinity.[9] From the perspective she adopts on other issues, it is clear also that she would have been extremely reluctant to identify personally with any tradition that was less than all-embracing in its claims, and that would in consequence have shut her off from humanity in its totality.

At the heart of her condemnation, however, lies her opposition to a certain concept of God, a God who is seen as powerful rather than good, and whose will can be discerned in the revelation of history. In some ways her criticism simply reiterates that developed in French thought from the Enlightenment onwards. In its expression as a confusion of the good and the necessary it is more personal to her. This confusion is in complete contrast to their distinction in the Greek world where, according to Simone Weil, misfortune is an inevitable part of the human condition and common to all, and it is difficult to see how, with her essentially Greek view of the world, Simone Weil could have had a different perspective on early Judaism. It is important to note that what she condemns is not the accounts of massacres in the Old Testament — the *Iliad* is also full of atrocities — rather it is the attitude that is revealed towards them. When Israel exterminates her enemies, the action is ordered and approved by God, and Israel is 'doing good': when Greeks and Trojans commit atrocities, they do so impelled by 'hard necessity'. The way in which the two traditions are mutually exclusive is illustrated clearly for her by the passage in the *Iliad* where Zeus takes his golden scales and, against his own preference, gives the victory to the Greeks. For Simone Weil this decision expresses the workings of necessity to which Zeus himself must submit, but Western Europe is so conditioned by the idea of an all-powerful God that Zeus' inability to influence the battle is interpreted as weakness on his part.

Simone Weil would not accept the accusation often levelled at her, that she misunderstood the dialectic within which the Jewish tradition developed, and that she did not take account of the interpretation of the Old Testament as the account of the evolution of a people, containing both their revolt against God and the exhortation to return to Him. The idea of a developing tradition is too close to moral relativism to be acceptable to Simone Weil, which is why she rejects totally the idea that an event or a custom should be judged in the light of the age, and that moral absolutes are inappropriate as guidelines. For her, absolute goodness is and always has been the same: 'It is as obvious that there are fluctuations in morals according to time and country as it is that the moral code issuing directly from mysticism is one, identical, unchangeable. . . . This moral code is unchangeable because it is a reflection of absolute good which is situated outside the world'.[10] It is inadequate to try and explain, therefore, the historical 'mistakes' of the Church, such as the Inquisition, by invoking the spirit of the age which weighed upon the Church itself as upon its individual members. Simone Weil points out that people considered as saints approved the Crusades and the Inquisition. She cannot help believing them to have been wrong. If on this point she sees more clearly than they did, they must have been blinded by something very powerful. 'This something', she concludes, 'is the Church as a social entity' (*AD* 22).

To express this 'something', and collective power in general, Simone Weil turns again to the Greek world, to Plato's image of society as 'the Great Beast' ('le gros animal'), whom his masters (society's leaders) try to tame by studying his moods and habits. Simone Weil makes this into a symbol of universal significance, and she uses it throughout her writings to indicate the dangers inherent in the social element, and the idolatry of society which so often results. The principal danger, as she sees it, is that, although the Beast belongs exclusively to the realm of necessity, its power is such that one tends to see in it an absolute. In her commentary on a passage of Plato's *Republic*, she notes two points of significance: firstly, that the opinions of the Beast are not necessarily contrary to truth. They are, however, essentially 'opinions', judgements made in response to social pressures and thus, even if these opinions are sometimes in accordance with truth, they are completely divorced from it. As Simone Weil says: 'If one feels like stealing but refrains from doing so, there is a great difference between refraining through obedience to the Great Beast or through obedience to God'.[11]

The second point concerns the difficulty of being truly objective in our interpretation of events in the world. It is almost impossible to discern the real motives for an action, she says, because we are so totally under the influence of the Great Beast. In fact, everything which goes to make up our education consists of things which have at one time or another been approved by the Great Beast. This is particularly clear in what we call history. 'The men whose names have come down to us have been made famous by the Great Beast. Those whom it does not make famous remain unknown both by their contemporaries and by posterity'.[12] The idolatry of history is inevitable under the influence of the Great Beast.

Once again we can see how the absolute nature of Simone Weil's thought gives it a pessimistic ring when applied to society as it necessarily exists. The incarnations of the Beast are many and various, but the inspiration which renders a human being capable of discerning it remains the same. The approach is as coherent as it is without compromise, and is at the root of most of the negative judgements Simone Weil makes on various civilisations throughout the ages. The Beast represents for her the elevation of society into an absolute, which is then judged without reference to anything exterior, so that in a very real sense nothing but the collective exists. This is the characteristic of what Simone Weil calls totalitarianism, and here of course her usage is in line with what we have become accustomed to designate by that term. The Beast represents the totality of collective values and the destruction of the individual. Its main concern is existence, and since the existence of anything else is intolerable to it, its own existence involves infinite expansion, a total hold over the lives of its subjects.

Expansion in such a context is clearly not simply territorial. As we know from modern manifestations of totalitarianism, its most essential feature is the way in which the minds of the members of the society in question are taken over. It is as much intellectual and spiritual as it is physical, and it is not surprising therefore that Simone Weil should accuse the medieval Church of having been 'a totalitarian Great Beast', the spirit of which has come down to the present day. We have already seen the intensity of Simone Weil's dialogue with the Church in the latter years of her life; if she remained to the end on the threshold, refusing the communion which one part of her so ardently desired, it was largely because of the Church as a social phenomenon. She saw in St Thomas's definition of faith as submission to the Church the iron hand of totalitarianism applied to the intellect: 'The unconditional and global adherence to all that the Church teaches, has taught and will teach, which St Thomas called faith, is not faith but social idolatry', she declares.[13] In her view the medieval Church established itself as an 'earthly God', the equivalent from all points of view to the national God of Judaism. This worship of the social element was all the more dangerous in the case of the Church in that it was 'a society with divine claims', which contained 'an imitation of goodness' (*C*2 203). It operated therefore on the spiritual as well as the temporal plane, using physical persecution and excommunication as weapons to exact conformity. Simone Weil found spiritual persecution even more reprehensible than physical: the use of the anathema, by which the Church excluded a member for holding heretical opinions, was for her an abuse of its true role, which was to be 'a depository for the sacraments and keeper of the sacred texts'. Dogma must be defined by the Church, but without the exercise of sanctions (*C*3 282). In any case, it cannot constrain the intelligence to adhere to dogma; only attention is voluntary, and it is thus the only obligation (*LR* 64). The Church can warn against the practical consequences of certain speculations of the intelligence, but it cannot suppress them (*AD* 46). It has the right to condemn as heretical certain opinions which reduce the value of the mysteries of Christianity (for example refusing the inseparability of the human and the divine natures in Christ), and can in this case prevent the teaching of such opinions within the Church. But it should on no account exclude from the Church those that hold and teach these opinions.

Simone Weil's strong views on the role of the Church are yet another illustration of the importance and uniqueness of the individual human mind in man's approach to the universe in which he finds himself. It is in the power of the mind that the individual's superiority over the collectivity lies. In the domain of thought, 'the individual surpasses the collectivity as something surpasses nothing, for thought takes place only in a mind alone with itself; collectivities do not think at all'.[14] Small wonder, then, that she had such difficulties coming to terms with the authoritarian approach to the faith which the Church has often displayed, and certainly continued to display in France at that time. One is tempted to feel that she would have been much more at home in a faith such as Buddhism where access to the truth is not mediated by the authority of a Church. In Buddhism, after all, truth is obtainable by anyone who makes the necessary effort of attention, and that was exactly Simone Weil's approach. But, although attracted by certain aspects of oriental religion, Simone Weil held firmly that to change one's religion was as dangerous for a sense of spiritual identity as changing one's language was for linguistic identity. The sacraments she desired were the Christian sacraments, and the personal contact in her mystical experiences was with Christ and not with the Buddha.

It remains true that the ideal role she conceived for the Church has very little in common with the medieval Church, with its huge temporal power which it was obliged to wield according to the laws of power, by temporal means. Simone Weil sees the reasons for what she considers to be this aberration in the very origins of the Church. As far as she is concerned, the Roman Empire took over from Israel, and the Church, in turn, took over from the Empire. Of all the civilisations that attract Simone Weil's criticism, it is perhaps in respect of the Roman Empire that her condemnation is most absolute. In fact, in her view, the Roman Empire hardly deserved to be called a civilisation at all but, since it is at the heart of modern Europe, it has influenced and, she would add, polluted, the whole of Western culture, coming down to modern times partly through the Church. Simone Weil maybe overestimates the extent to which the early Church was Roman, but the position of the Church under Constantine was very similar to that of the Roman religion in the pre-Christian period. Constantine was, after all, a Roman Emperor, none the less Roman for being Christian. The moment of Rome's 'baptism' marks the end for Simone Weil of the true Christian spirit, and the totalitarian elements in the Church are due to that alliance.

The same criticisms that Simone Weil levelled at Israel are directed at the Roman Empire. It was 'a totalitarian and grossly materialistic regime, founded on the exclusive worship of the State'. It was not so much a question of worshipping God through the intermediary of the State, rather one of making the State into a God, thus attempting to suppress all thought of the true God and to allow only the power of the State as object of worship (*CS* 171). Again, social idolatry brings about the reduction of God to the social element: 'The Roman Empire was ... idolatrous. The idol was the State. One worshipped the Emperor. All forms of religious life being subordinate to these, none of them was able to rise above idolatry'.[15] It comes as no suprise to see Simone Weil using the identification made in the Apocalypse between Rome and the Beast: 'Rome is the materialistic Great Beast, worshipping only itself' (*C3* 106).

It is in this light that Simone Weil exposes the so-called tolerance of the Romans towards other religions. In fact, she says, such tolerance is deceptive, because they tolerated only those political and spiritual manifestations which could not harm the central authority. In terms of religion, they tolerated 'all those religious practices which were devoid of spiritual content'. For example, they accepted freely the cult of Mithra, which Simone

Weil describes, perhaps over-harshly, as a 'fake orientalism for snobs and idle women' (*E* 232)! The Druids, however, representing a much more considerable force, were exterminated, she says, 'for the crime of patriotism'. Nothing which was rich in spiritual content survived. Simone Weil rejects totally the idea of Rome as a civilising force, and its corollary, that there was no civilisation worthy of that name prior to their arrival in those lands conquered by the Romans. For her, it is a case of history being written by the conquerors: concerning the Romans, she says, we possess nothing but what the Romans themselves or their Greek slaves wrote (*E* 192). Why should we doubt their testimony? We have no motive for doing so, since it is not the Carthaginians who award prizes for scholarship or elect Sorbonne professors.

One of Simone Weil's most sustained presentations of Rome is contained in the long three-part article 'Quelques réflexions sur les origines de l'hitlérisme', to which I have already referred, where she makes a detailed comparison between the spirit of the Roman Empire and that of Nazi Germany. It is an interesting and at times very convincing parallel: she shows to what extent their external policies were similar, based as they were on expansion and domination, and using methods without discrimination provided they were effective. She compares the lack of honour frequent among the Romans in their relationship with foreign countries with Hitler's disregard for treaties and agreements which did not suit him. She refutes Hitler's idea of an 'eternal Germany', remaining essentially the same over the centuries, by indicating the huge differences between the Germans in the time of the Roman Empire — free, hospitable, honest — and contemporary Nazis. It is true that she depends largely for her sources on Tacitus, who saw in the barbarous Germans an echo of the earlier dignity of Rome, contrasting the latter with the vice and indulgence of his own age. It is also true that Simone Weil had a tendency to idealise barbarians, and in general peoples who had not been touched by Western civilisation (while mourning the fact that there are no barbarians left, since we have 'civilised' them all). But her comparison between the Roman temperament, especially under the Republic, and that of the Nazis, seems accurate: they were noted for 'order, discipline and endurance, obstinacy and conscientiousness in their work' (*EH* 40). We do not see these parallels, however, unless they are pointed out to us.

We get indignant, and rightly so, over cruelties perpetrated in our own age, but time has softened the brutalities of earlier times. We are therefore scandalised, she suggests, by the deportation of peasants in the Southern Tyrol and in Eastern Europe, but these do not bring to mind the deportations which Virgil laments in his 'First Eclogue'.

Such is the power of the Great Beast that neither do we recognise brutality when it forms part of our own heritage. The greatness of Napoleon, for example, is of the same kind as that of Hitler (we should remember again that Simone Weil was writing this at the beginning of the war, when only limited information was available concerning what was happening under Hitler). We like to claim, she says, that Napoleon propagated, weapons at the ready, the ideas of freedom and equality proclaimed by the French Revolution. What he chiefly propagated, however, was the idea of the centralised State, the State as sole source of authority and exclusive object of worship (*EH* 13–14). Not that Napoleon invented the idea of the centralised state: Napoleon and even Louis XIV, in their admiration for the reign of Augustus, are only harking back to the Roman model. If their efforts were not always crowned with success, she says, that fact should be put down to a lack of talent rather than an excess of scruple. The real creator of the modern State was, however, Richelieu rather than Louis. Simone Weil sees in Richelieu a kind of watershed in the development of attitudes to power. Before Richelieu, she says, one could speak in tones of religious attachment concerning the public good, the country, the King, the lord. Richelieu was the first to adopt the principle that whoever exercised a public function owes his entire loyalty in the exercise of that function not to the public, not to the King, but to the State and to nothing else. By thus transforming the State, whose reality is founded in this world, into an absolute, Richelieu committed the crime of idolatry: the temptation of temporal power offered by the Devil and refused by Christ, was accepted by Richelieu. The State is not a natural object of veneration: but the Great Beast is totalitarian in its demands, and since in the end it destroys all opposition, it takes to itself the human need for an object of worship. 'The State is a cold thing, which cannot be loved; but it kills and weakens anything that could be; one is thus forced to love it, because there is nothing else'.[16] Richelieu began the immense work of centralisation, killing in France everything that was not Paris, from which France is still emerging with difficulty.

Worship of the State is an example of social idolatry for Simone Weil: but in her view it colours at the same time all social relationships. Her perspective on the seventeenth century, the great century of Louis XIV, is an original one, in that it brings into question the more or less automatic reverence for the great figures of that century with which French people are brought up. Simone Weil is particularly harsh towards the new servility which is a direct product of the idolatry of the State fostered by Richelieu. Corneille, whom she detested, was in her view a particularly glaring example of the way in which writers had to flatter the King in order to be accepted, and she attributes this defect in him to his admiration for Ancient Rome. Corneille, she says, reduced the relationship between sovereign and subject to the level of slavery, and the concept of patriotism to idolatry. Patriotism as it is taught through the medium of writers such as Corneille, and inherited from the Romans, has no connection with that compassion for one's native land which Simone Weil considered to be true patriotism. Joan of Arc whom, as we have seen, she treats with a certain suspicion, reflected this when she said she had 'feelings of pity for the kingdom of France' (E 147).

Simone Weil did not, of course, restrict herself to finding instances of social idolatry in history: the Great Beast was alive and well in her own time. We have already seen how strongly critical she was of the various manifestations of the totalitarian State, her condemnation of Soviet Russia and of the new Fascist regimes: her analysis of Rome is pursued mainly with a view to showing the similarities with Hitler's Germany. Towards the end of her life, her main preoccupation apart from the war which no one could ignore, was the situation of the French colonies, at a time when few people envisaged that a change of status for the component parts of the French Empire was either possible or desirable. Imperialism is, of course, a classic example of the functioning of the Great Beast, based as it is on limitless expansion. The case of Cecil Rhodes, who was seized with horror at the idea that there were geographical limits to his otherwise boundless ambitions, is a striking illustration of this. Expansion is considered not only as a means of acquiring material possessions, but as a good in itself. As Simone Weil says, in this perspective 'the past is only the story of the growth of France, and it is accepted that this growth is always a good in all respects'.[17] The question of prestige is in the end more important than simple financial gain.

The phenomenon of 'setting aside', which I commented on above, is also present in imperialism, so that certain things are considered outside all relationships and not questioned. Imperialism is totalitarian by its very nature; especially in the case of French imperialism, it is always the imposition of a foreign culture on a subject people, in the belief that the imposed culture is the only valid one. France has always willingly assimilated her colonised peoples, provided that they totally accepted French culture, creating the phenomenon of 'black Frenchmen' that is so characteristic of the French system. Provided a black child in Senegal or Niger or any other of the French colonies was prepared to submit himself totally to the French educational system, a bright future lay in front of him if he were sufficiently gifted; a highly-paid post in Paris was by no means an idle dream. Such a policy, however, results inevitably in a total uprooting of the colonised people. As Simone Weil demonstrates, a system which in her day required little Polynesians to repeat mechanically 'Our ancestors the Gauls had blond hair', could produce only a refusal and a destruction of all that does not emanate from the foreign regime (*E* 47).

Simone Weil is also bitterly critical of the methods by which colonial expansion took place, evaluated as they were in relation to the aim pursued rather than judged in themselves on moral grounds. She uses the same terms to describe the way the French acquired certain territories, the behaviour of the Romans in their pursuit of Empire, and Hitler's use of treachery and bad faith in his foreign policy. The essays she wrote on Morocco, one entitled 'Le Maroc, ou la prescription en matière de vol' ('Morocco, or instructions regarding theft') (*EH* 331–5), and the other 'Un peu d'histoire à propos du Maroc' ('A little history concerning Morocco'),[18] are relevant examples. In these essays she outlines the facts of France's seizure of Morocco, and denounces the way in which the Act of Algeciras, establishing France's rights in Morocco, had been violated. The provocation of Germany by this act, she claims, was not irrelevant to the outbreak of the First World War.

From this necessarily brief survey of Simone Weil's attitudes to history and to society in general, certain features stand out. One is free to accept or to reject her interpretations of individual historical facts, and to have reservations on the partiality of some of her judgements. She certainly lacks 'objectivity' in her passionate evaluations of certain historical phenomena, and leaves aside details which professional historians would claim to be significant. Her approach remains nevertheless an entirely coherent one. Starting from the radical distinction between the domain of absolute good and that of necessity in which history takes place, she demonstrates that, in almost every case where men have fallen into barbarity, frequently convinced at the same time that they were doing good, they have been blinded by the power of a collectivity which they considered by mistake as an absolute. Idolatry is thus nothing other than that attempt to embody the absolute in society, to forget the gulf so difficult to maintain between the absolute and the relative, and the disasters of history are the account of that idolatry. As she herself observes, 'the object of the real crime of idolatry is always something analogous to the State'.[19]

Notes

1. *PSO* 48: 'Connaître la divinité seulement comme puissance et non comme bien, c'est l'idolâtrie, et peu importe alors qu'on ait un Dieu ou plusieurs'.
2. *CS* 171: 'On ne peut pas se mettre devant un morceau de bois sculpté et lui dire: "Tu as fait le ciel et la terre"'.
3. *OL* 65: 'Marx a prétendu "remettre sur ses pieds" la dialectique hégélienne, qu'il accusait d'être "sens dessus dessous"; il a substitué la matière à l'esprit comme moteur de l'histoire; mais par un paradoxe extraordinaire, il a conçu l'histoire, à partir de cette rectification, comme s'il attribuait à la matière ce qui est l'essence même de l'esprit, une perpétuelle aspiration au mieux'.
4. *C*2 256: 'Tout ce qui est couvert du prestige de la chose sociale est mis dans un autre lieu que le reste et soustrait à certains rapports'.
5. *C*3 66: 'La grande erreur des Marxistes et de tout le XIXe siècle a été de croire qu'en marchant tout droit devant soi, on monte dans les airs'.

6. *PSO* 51: 'La notion même de peuple élu est incompatible avec la connaissance du vrai Dieu'.
7. *PSO* 50: '[Moïse] voulait apparaître comme l'envoyé d'un Dieu puissant qui fait des promesses temporelles'.
8. *SG* 41: 'Les Hébreux voyaient dans le malheur le signe du péché et par suite un motif légitime de mépris; ils regardaient leurs ennemis vaincus comme étant en horreur à Dieu même et condamnés à expier des crimes, ce qui rendait la cruauté permise et même indispensable'.
9. For a discussion of some of the similarities between her thought and that of two other modern Jewish thinkers, see Florence de Lussy, 'Simone Weil: Confrontation avec deux grandes figures juives contemporaines: Martin Buber et Emmanuel Lévinas', *Revue de la Bibliothèque Nationale*, 6e année, no. 20, été 1986, pp. 17–42.
10. *OL* 211: 'Autant les fluctuations de la morale selon les temps et les pays sont évidentes, autant aussi il est évident que la morale qui procède directement de la mystique est une, identique, inaltérable. . . . Cette morale est inaltérable parce qu'elle est un reflet du bien absolu qui est situé hors de ce monde'.
11. *SG* 91: 'Si on a envie de voler et qu'on se retienne, il y a une grosse différence entre se retenir par obéissance au gros animal ou par obéissance à Dieu'.
12. Ibid.: 'Les hommes dont le nom est parvenu jusqu'à nous ont été rendus célèbres par le gros animal. Ceux qu'il ne rend pas célèbres restent inconnus et de leurs contemporains et de la postérité'.
13. *CS* 82: 'L'adhésion inconditionnée et globale à tout ce que l'Eglise enseigne, a enseigné et enseignera, que saint Thomas nomme la foi, n'est pas de la foi, mais de l'idolâtrie sociale'.
14. *OL* 130: 'L'individu dépasse la collectivité autant que quelque chose dépasse rien, car la pensée ne se forme que dans un esprit se trouvant seul en face de lui-même; les collectivités ne pensent point'.
15. *AD* 184: 'L'Empire romain était . . . idolâtre. L'idole était l'Etat. On adorait l'empereur. Toutes les formes de vie religieuse devant être subordonnées à celle-là, aucune d'elles ne pouvait s'élever au-dessus de l'idolâtrie'.
16. *E* 102: 'L'Etat est une chose froide qui ne peut pas être aimée; mais il tue et abolit tout ce qui pourrait l'être; ainsi on est forcé de l'aimer, parce qu'il n'y a que lui'.
17. *E* 121: 'Le passé n'est que l'histoire de la croissance de la France, et il est admis que cette croissance est toujours un bien à tous égards'.
18. *Syndicats* (Paris), 17, 4.2.37, pp. 3ff. Neither essay on Morocco is available in English translation.
19. *E* 103: 'L'objet du véritable crime d'idolâtrie est toujours quelque chose d'analogue à l'Etat'.

3 The Need for Roots

So far the conclusions Simone Weil draws from her approach to society seem to have been almost entirely negative. She sets her readers endlessly on guard against the power of the collectivity to absorb and stifle all that is most precious in a human being, she writes of society 'eating' its members, and the very image of the Great Beast which I have just been considering gives a clear impression of Simone Weil's deep mistrust of the social element, as well as of her view of its power. Potentially, however, she has a more positive judgement of what society can be to its members, when its organisation corresponds to certain clearly-defined principles, seldom taken account of and therefore rarely put into practice in contemporary or earlier civilisations. She has a clear idea of how things could be, but her pessimism regarding the contemporary scene is such that her vision of a more enlightened society, supported by the few examples of civilisations in history which have conformed to this vision, frequently takes second place to a criticism of what is wrong in the world around her. She is in some ways the archetypal Jewish prophet whose role is to castigate and warn of disaster, rather than produce a blueprint of a future society in all its detail. Thus the greater part of *L'Enracinement* (*The Need for Roots*), her most sustained piece of writing on society, first published in 1949, is devoted not to *enracinement* but to *déracinement*, an analysis of why and how society has become 'uprooted'. Even the section entitled 'l'enracinement' concentrates to a great extent on those factors which prevent *enracinement*.

This text furnishes an account of Simone Weil's most important ideas on the reorganisation of society and, taken with the other essays written in London and published as the *Ecrits de Londres et dernières lettres*, forms a very complete picture of her social philosophy at its most mature, written as all these texts were within months of her death.[1] The fact that they are circumstantial writings does not lessen the universal nature of their preoccupations. Although they were produced in response to the various reports and suggestions coming out of France at the time, Simone Weil seldom limited herself to the precise and practical

— and ultimately restricted — object of these reports, and her employers in the civil section of the Free French in London were frequently dismayed at the scope of her ideas, which went far beyond what they wanted. She saw clearly that what was needed after the war was not simply to pick up the threads dropped in 1940, but a complete re-thinking of French society based on a clear understanding of what had gone wrong. In her view, public life in France had been dead a long time when the Germans marched in: it was precisely because of this that there had been no effective reaction to the oppressor.

Simone Weil's determination to get to the origin of the malaise in French society gives much of her thinking in *L'Enracinement* a radically new feel. The opening sentence: 'The notion of obligation takes precedence over that of rights, which is subordinate and relative to it',[2] dispenses with several centuries of thinking on the fundamental principles of social organisation, including, of course, all the national and international charters for the protection of human freedoms from the American Declaration of Independence and the French Revolutionary Declaration of Human Rights onwards. She criticises the notion of rights on two grounds: firstly, a right is worthless except in conjunction with its corresponding obligation; it is of no use to me to have rights if no one else recognises them. Secondly, and more importantly in Simone Weil's eyes, rights belong to an inferior order, and are always conditioned by particular circumstances. The notion of rights is a legal one (in French *le droit* means both 'right' and 'the law'), and is linked to that of quantity, exchange, property. It comes to us straight from the Romans, she says, and the principal objects over which they claimed rights were other human beings, their slaves and subject populations. In the Greek world different principles applied: whereas the Romans had rights, among the Greeks justice was at the heart of relationships between people. Justice is based on mutual consent, and the cry of someone suffering injustice is 'Why am I being hurt?' The notion of rights, being based on property, produces a different cry: 'Why has he got more than I have?' (*EL* 38). The notion of obligation is unconditional, since it is situated on a higher plane than that of rights; the only difficulty lies in grasping the theoretical basis for the obligation towards one's fellow-beings, and then finding practical expression for it. The possession of rights always contains the possibility of making good or bad use of them, whereas obligations are always and everywhere on the side of goodness and justice (*E* 235).

To find Simone Weil's clearest and most sustained analysis of the foundation of obligations, we must turn again to the admirable 'Etude pour une déclaration des obligations envers l'être humain' ('Study for a declaration of obligations towards the human being'), which we have had occasion to consider in the context of Simone Weil's fundamental dualism (see Chapter 1, note 1 above). The 'reality situated outside the world', in other words, goodness, becomes the source of obligation in the following way: whoever recognises this other reality recognises also the link between it and every human being without exception by virtue of his desire for goodness. The recognition of this link forms the basis for the respect to be shown towards every person as something sacred. But because the link belongs to a higher reality, it is impossible to express this respect in direct fashion. It is, however, possible to express it indirectly through the needs of people in this world, the earthly needs of body and soul. It is this possibility of expressing indirect respect towards fellow human beings that is the basis of obligation. She summarises it thus:

> Whoever has his attention and love turned in fact towards that reality outside the world recognises at the same time that he is bound, in both public and private life, by the unique and perpetual obligation, according to his responsibilities and to the extent of his power, to alleviate all those privations of the soul and the body capable of destroying or mutilating the earthly life of a human being whoever he may be.[3]

The complex association of the highly abstract with the concrete noticeable here is entirely typical of Simone Weil. It is characteristic that on the one hand she places 'another reality', inaccessible to human faculties but guarantor of all goodness in the world, and on the other the real human needs of flesh and blood individuals. Another characteristic that is immediately obvious is the universality of her pronouncement, both in space and time: all human beings have a desire for the good, no matter what their intellectual or economic status is, and all have the same basic needs towards which we have absolute obligations.

1. Simone with her father, Dr Bernard Weil, Mayenne (1915–1916)

2. Mme Selma Weil, Simone's mother

3. Simone with her brother André, Knokke-le-Zoute (1922)

4. Spain (1936)

5. Marseille (Spring 1941)

6. Simone Weil in New York (1942)

Love

Love bade me welcome; yet my soul drew back,
    Guiltie of dust and sin.
But quick-ey'd Love, observing me grow slack
    From my first entrance in,
Drew nearer to me, sweetly questioning
    If I lack'd anything.

A guest, I answer'd, worthy to be here.
    Love said, you shall be he.
I, the unkinde, ungrateful? Ah, my deare,
    I cannot look on thee.
Love took my hand and smiling did reply:
    Who made the eyes but I?

Truth, Lord, but I have marr'd them. Let my shame
    Go where it doth deserve.
And know you not, says Love, who bore the blame?
    My deare, then I will serve.
You must sit down, says Love, and taste my meat.
    So I did sit and eat

7. Manuscript copy by Simone Weil of George Herbert's poem 'Love'

8. Extract from the 'Factory Journal'

gagné à cette expérience? Le sentiment que je ne possède aucun droit, quel qu'il soit, à quoi que ce soit (attention de ne pas le perdre). La capacité de me suffire moralement à moi-même, de vivre dans cet état d'humiliation latente perpétuelle sans me sentir humiliée à mes propres yeux; de goûter intensément chaque instant de liberté ou de camaraderie, comme s'il devait être éternel. Un contact direct avec la vie....

J'ai failli être brisée. Je l'ai presque été — mon courage, mon le sentiment de ma dignité ont été à peu près brisés pendant une période dont le souvenir m'humilierait, si ce n'était que je n'en ai à proprement parlé pas conservé le souvenir. Je me levais avec angoisse, j'allais à l'usine avec crainte ; je travaillais comme une esclave; la pause de midi était un déchirement; rentrée à 5 h3/4, préoccupée aussitôt de dormir assez (ce que je ne faisais pas) et de me réveiller assez tôt. Le temps était un poids intolérable. La crainte — la peur — de ce qui allait suivre ne cessait d'étreindre le cœur que le samedi après-midi et le dimanche matin. Et l'objet de la crainte, c'étaient les ordres (~~...~~)

Le sentiment de la dignité personnelle tel qu'il a été fabriqué par la société est brisé. Il faut s'en forger un autre (bien que l'épuisement éteigne la conscience de sa propre faculté de penser!). S'efforcer de conserver cet autre.

On se rend compte enfin de sa propre importance.

La classe de ceux qui ne <u>comptent pas</u> — dans aucune situation — aux yeux de personne... et qui ne <u>compteront pas</u>, jamais, quoi qu'il arrive (en dépit du dernier vers de la 1ère strophe de l'Internationale).

9. Simone's conclusions on her factory experience

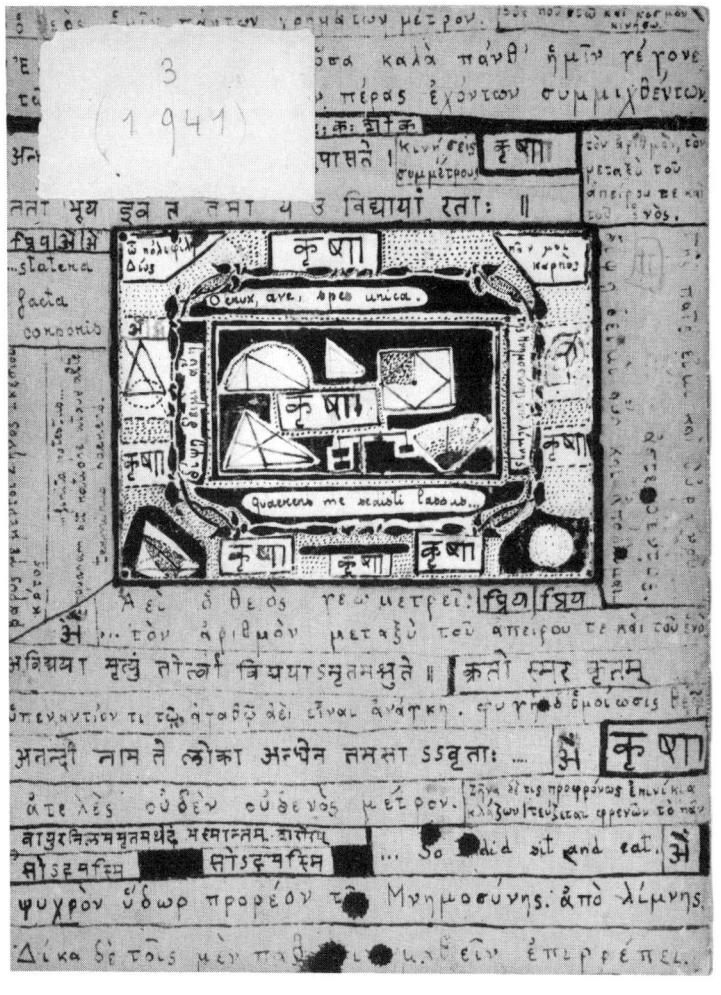

10. Cover of one of Simone's Notebooks (1941)

Nuit obscure — Nuit obscure dans l'apprentissage. L'apprenti qui se dit qu'il n'y arrivera jamais. À étudier.

Peut-être l'homme doit-il (chaque fois, jusqu'à l'état suprême?) passer par l'épreuve de la durée perpétuelle (enfer) avant d'avoir accès à l'éternité?

« Par l'ignorance ayant franchi la mort, par le savoir il mange l'immortalité. »

« Par le non-devenir ayant franchi la mort, par le devenir il mange l'immortalité. »

Franchir la mort par l'ignorance, cela désigne peut-être la « nuit obscure » ? C'est peut-être ce sentiment du mal perpétuel?

Le travail manuel. Le temps qui entre dans le corps. Qu'il soit régulier et inexorable. Mais varié, comme les jours et les saisons.
Par le travail l'homme se fait matière comme le Christ par l'eucharistie. Le travail est comme une mort.

Il faut passer par la mort — que le vieil homme meure. Mais la mort n'est pas un suicide. Il faut être tué; subir la pesanteur, le poids du monde. L'univers pesant sur les reins d'un être humain, quoi d'étonnant qu'il ait mal?

Le travail est comme une mort s'il est sans stimulant. Agir en renonçant aux fruits de l'action. Le faire le peut aussi.

Travailler — si l'on est épuisé — c'est devenir soumis au temps de la même manière que la matière. La pensée est contrainte de passer d'un instant au suivant. C'est là obéir.

11. Page from one of the Notebooks (1941)

être, c'est à dire ~~sous~~ aucune chose ~~inconditionnée~~ particulière. Vouloir les choses particulières sous condition. Vouloir la mie si elle doit être un bien, la mort si..., la joie si..., la douleur si... ; et cela sachant que nous ignorons ce qu'est le bien.

En tout ~~à~~ vouloir, quelqu'il soit, par delà l'objet particulier, vouloir à vide, vouloir le vide. Car c'est un vide pour nous que ce bien que nous ne pourrons ni nous représenter ni définir. Mais ce vide est plus pour nous que tous les ~~biens~~ pleins.

Si on en arrive là, on est tiré d'affaire, car Dieu comble le vide.

Il ne s'agit nullement d'un processus intellectuel au sens où nous entendons aujourd'hui intellectuel. L'intelligence n'a rien à trouver, elle a à déblayer. Elle est bonne aux tâches serviles.

Savoir que rien de ce qu'on touche, entend, voit, etc., rien de ce qu'on se représente, rien de ce qu'on pense n'est le bien. Si on pense Dieu, ce n'est pas le bien non plus. Tout ce que nous pensons est imparfait comme nous, et l'imparfait n'est pas le bien. [Ce que nous faisons, plus encore.]

Le bien est pour nous un néant, puisque aucune chose n'est bonne. Mais ce néant n'est pas non-être, n'est pas irréel. Tout ce qui existe comparé à lui est irréel. Ce ~~ne~~ néant est au moins aussi réel que nous. Car notre être même n'est pas autre chose que ce besoin du bien. Le bien absolu est tout entier dans ce besoin. ~~Nous ne~~ Mais nous ne pouvons pas aller l'y prendre.

Nous pouvons seulement aimer à vide. Mais comme nous avons besoin d'objets sensibles, nous aimons les ~~des~~ choses et les êtres finis, limités qui nous entourent. Mais non pas en tant que dignes d'amour. En tant qu'indignes de d'amour. "Celui qui ne hait pas...." L'amour sans objets sensibles est imaginaire ("Si tu n'aimes pas ton

---

12. Page from one of the Notebooks (1942)

Déclaration fondamentale des obligations envers tous les êtres humains

---

Préambule

Il y a hors de cet univers, au delà de ce que les facultés humaines peuvent saisir, une réalité à laquelle correspond dans le cœur humain l'exigence de bien ~~absolu~~ total qui se trouve en tout homme. De cette réalité découle tout ce qui est bien ici-bas. C'est d'elle que procède toute obligation.

Sur elle est fondée l'obligation ~~~~ qui engage chaque homme envers tous les êtres humains sans aucune exception.

Cette obligation est celle de satisfaire aux besoins terrestres de l'âme et du corps de chaque être humain autant qu'il est possible.

Les besoins d'un être humain, quel qu'il soit, sans aucune exception, doivent être considérés avec le même degré d'attention que ceux de n'importe quel autre être humain.

L'objet de la vie publique est de mettre autant que possible toutes les formes du pouvoir aux mains de ceux qui savent quelle est l'obligation de chaque homme envers tous les êtres humains et qui consentent réellement à être liés

13. Beginning of a draft for the 'Declaration of obligations'
(London 1943)

This has always been the case, she says: 'Human conscience has never varied on this point. Thousands of years ago, the Egyptians thought that a soul could not be justified after death unless it could say "I have let no one suffer hunger"'.[4]

Because the human physical need for food is the most fundamental one of all, Simone Weil takes it as a model for all the others. A considerable part of *L'Enracinement* is devoted to an analysis of the various needs of mankind, in particular of course the need for 'roots', and for each need is implied the corresponding obligation. She divides them into physical and spiritual needs, while underlining that they are all, none the less, 'earthly'. She also indicates the way in which needs can be distinguished from mere desires: needs, she says, are limited; I need food, but when I have had enough I need to stop eating, whereas desire is unlimited; a miser never has enough gold (E 16–17). A second characteristic, linked to the first, is that needs can be distinguished in pairs: we need exercise, but also rest. This way of categorising needs helps again to distinguish them from mere fancies.

Taking physical needs as self-evident, Simone Weil then reviews a number of the needs of the soul, showing again her sense both of the concrete situation and of the universal nature of these needs. Frequently she indicates needs which are not often identified as such, or which are presented differently in traditional thinking on the subject, and this is very much a result of her approaching the question from the point of view of needs rather than rights. Human beings have need of order, for example: but what would it mean to say that I have a *right* to order? The very notion of the need for order is framed in terms of obligations, in fact: order is 'a network of relationships such that no one is forced to violate strict obligations in order to carry out other obligations' (E 15). The fact that Simone Weil puts the need for order, defined thus, as the first need of the soul is very likely a result of the wartime situation in which she found herself at the time of writing *L'Enracinement*: in such a situation incompatible obligations loom large, especially when one's homeland is occupied by an enemy power and when impossible choices become a daily source of anguish. Although she does not make a direct comparison at this point, it is clear that her idea of order is far removed from that of the *Pax Romana*, which she describes elsewhere as an imitation of order, brought about by the destruction of all genuine local life and culture.

Corresponding to the need for order is the need for freedom. In line with other thinking on the subject, she sees freedom only in a context of limits to freedom. But her stipulation that the usefulness of these limits and the necessity for them be understood is more personally hers, as is her desire that the authority imposing the limits should be accepted (her word is 'loved') by the population, and not regarded as foreign or enemy. In another essay written in London, 'Luttons-nous pour la justice?' ('Are we fighting for justice?'), she significantly defines freedom as 'the real possibility of giving consent' (*EL* 51). I will return to this concept when I look at those societies which Simone Weil considers to have been genuinely 'rooted'. For the moment it is sufficient to note that when Simone Weil evokes the need for obedience, she does so entirely in terms of consent. Obedience without consent is nothing, so much so that to subject human beings to constraint and cruelty is in her view to deprive them of two forms of vital nourishment, freedom and obedience.

Among other needs that Simone Weil considers basic to the human being, it is worth evoking equality, because of the way in which she sees it working as a two-way process. The upward movement which allows a child of modest origin to aspire to high position is valid only if there is a corresponding downward movement: to the extent to which it is possible for the son of a farm-hand to become one day a minister, it should also be possible for the son of a minister to become a farm-hand. This however, can create dangerous social flux, and Simone Weil recommends to counterbalance it a system of proportion between equality and inequality, so that responsibility would always be in proportion to power. Thus a boss guilty of incapacity or irregularity towards his workforce should suffer far more in real terms than an unskilled worker guilty of the same offences towards his boss.

The notion of punishment being apportioned according to social rank was a very important one for Simone Weil. The very fact that she envisages punishment as a human need is of interest, since it is not normally so considered. Simone Weil viewed a criminal as someone who had by his crime put himself outside the network of eternal obligations towards the rest of humanity.

Punishment was a way, the only way, of reintegrating him, fully if the punishment was consented to, otherwise imperfectly. It is a process for 'providing pure good to people who do not desire it; the art of punishment is the art of awaking in criminals the desire for pure good by pain or even by death'.[5] In fact, it is the only means society has of showing respect for a criminal. But she recognises that punishment was generally only a degraded image of this ideal, claiming that the penal code was only 'a process of constraint through terror' (E 25), and that repressive justice as practised currently was more hideous than crime itself.

The same gap between the ideal and the practice is noticeable when Simone Weil considers freedom of opinion as a human need. The scheme for such freedom would indeed need ideal conditions to be put into action. She in fact only claims complete freedom for the intelligence when it is speculating in a theoretical fashion, removed from all concern for practical application. Then, however, she demands total and absolute freedom of a kind which, in an imperfect world, it would be very easy to abuse. For example, there should be a certain category of publication reserved for the arguments in favour of bad causes, these arguments being seen as a contribution to the debate on a question, and neither committing their author nor being presented as recommendations to readers. On the other hand, publications destined to influence public opinion and practical conduct were to be seen as acts, and subject to the same restraints as all acts — in other words, in this area, strict censorship was to operate. Simone Weil claims that distinction between the two areas is easy enough to establish if the will is there, but even so some of the distinctions she makes seem somewhat arbitrary. For example, the press in its entirety came into the second category. Much of contemporary literature also did, by virtue of the way in which writers have taken upon themselves the role of directors of conscience, even while claiming protection behind the label of 'art for art's sake'. When such writers abuse their power, by contributing to a corruption of a nation's moral atmosphere, for example, punishment should be severe. Why should André Gide's novels, which had such an impact on the youth of the time, claim immunity as 'art', she asks, when we imprison a lad who, influenced by Gide, throws someone out of a moving train? One can imagine Simone Weil's contribution to the present-day debate on the influence of the media, and television in particular, on the youth of today.

Even when the implementation of Simone Weil's particular form of censorship is doubtful, her intention remains clear: in every area she wanted to make people responsible for their words and actions, and the more power they exercise, the more responsibility they must show and the more they should be penalised for any misuse of their power.

The need for freedom of opinion is clearly related to that which she considers 'more sacred than any other', the need for truth, and it is here that she is in fact harshest towards those who refuse or omit to fulfil the need. Put briefly, she considered that it should be a crime to publish in any form material which could be shown to be false, whether deliberately or as an oversight. She envisages the setting up of special tribunals empowered to punish with public reprobation or, for frequent offenders, with prison or penal servitude, all proven instances of misleading the public where it could be avoided. In her mind are ordinary working people, who read books in the evening in order to instruct themselves, and who do not have time to go checking all the facts in a reference library. It is for such people that the sacred need for truth must be protected. Under the heading of protection of the truth Simone Weil also puts the need to be protected against propaganda, and here of course the whole political arena opens up, to which I will return later because of its wide implications. Advertising also, which could almost be the modern and most insidious incarnation of the Great Beast, with its collective values and its almost inevitable tendency to mislead, was to be severely restricted, and never allowed to touch the domain of thought.

From these relatively precisely defined 'needs of the soul', Simone Weil passes on to the one which occupies most of *L'Enracinement*, the need for *enracinement* itself, which she admits is the most difficult to define but none the less the most important.

> A human being has roots by his real, active and natural participation in the existence of a collectivity which preserves alive certain treasures from the past and certain premonitions regarding the future. [. . .] Every human being needs to have multiple roots. He needs to receive practically the whole of his moral, intellectual and spiritual life through the intermediary of those milieux in which he naturally participates.[6]

Every community is thus specific and unique, and the destruction of a community the loss of something irreplaceable. It is interesting that her conviction of the specificity of an individual culture does not lead her into the moral relativism of the nineteenth-century German Romantics, that of Herder, for example, whose emphasis on the *Volksgeist* enabled him to withhold moral judgement in respect of individual cultural and political manifestations: each society was to be viewed as an isolated entity, and no moral absolute could apply. On the contrary, as we have already seen, Simone Weil was convinced that cruelty and barbarity were to be judged as such no matter what age and society produced them.

It is hardly surprising if, in the war-torn Europe of the early months of 1943, when virtually every community was uprooted if not totally destroyed, Simone Weil should turn immediately from a definition of *enracinement* to an analysis of its opposite, *déracinement*, the process or state of being uprooted. She had a practical aim in mind, however, and that was to attempt to diagnose what had gone wrong in France in 1940. In her view, the uprooted state of the French nation was almost alone responsible for that defeat, even though this state resulted from a process which had been going on for centuries. The next hundred pages or so are a powerful if highly idiosyncratic view of French history and culture, in which many hitherto untouched heads roll and many sacred cows are slaughtered. There is also a long analysis of why working people have become uprooted, to which I shall return at a later stage.

At the heart of her criticism of French history lies the notion that what is transmitted habitually in the name of history is a sense of false greatness (E 187). History, she claims, is a mass of baseness and cruelty from which a few drops of purity shine out from time to time. This is partly because effectively there is not much purity on this earth, but also because in the nature of things it is the horrors that are transmitted. It is completely false, she says, to claim that a providential mechanism transmits what is best in any age to succeeding generations. On the contrary, under the pressure of the Great Beast, it is false greatness that is passed on. Most of what is genuinely great and pure simply disappears, because history is the record of relationships of force, and by definition the superior force always wins and transmits its version of events to the next age. She makes a nice distinction between people and groups who are definitively beaten, and those for whom it is only a temporary state: the latter, she claims, benefit from a certain sentimentality on the part of others that is in itself subject to force. Affliction has great prestige when the prestige of force is added to it; we take no notice of it when it is pure affliction. Why else did the post-1918 pacifists show so much more concern for Germany than for Austria? Why did the need for paid holidays seem so obvious in 1936 (after the victory of the Popular Front) and not at all in 1935? Why do people pay so much more attention to the needs of industrial than to those of agricultural workers? In history the same mechanism applies; defeat has a certain prestige and therefore interest when time has brought about some form of revenge.

An interesting by-product of this view of history lies in the necessary transformation of historical method. Simone Weil is clearly very sceptical regarding the so-called objectivity of the historian. The historian works on documents, and these certainly form part of the record; but because they are what has survived in a relationship of force, they are necessarily biased. To correct the balance, she sees a need to elaborate and use hypotheses that have no apparent foundation, and to read between the lines of existing documents, giving total and selfless attention to significant details. It would seem that what is necessary for the interpretation of history is not talent, but genius, in her definition of the term: the depersonalised desire for truth which has rid itself of the power of collective suggestion. On her terms, it is clear that there could never be many true historians.

It is indispensable, however, in Simone Weil's view, that scepticism regarding what is usually viewed as history should not preclude the fostering of a genuine patriotism. France must be its object, but an object 'to love not for its glory, its prestige, its brilliance, its conquests, its influence, its future expansion, but in itself, in its nakedness and its reality . . .'.[7] One might add that the situation in which Simone Weil and French people in general found themselves at the time *L'Enracinement* was written was an ideal one for displaying true patriotism. France had lost everything, apparently, and had been subject to a cruelly humiliating defeat. It was at that moment no longer possible to consider the country for its glory, its power, its prestige. Simone Weil's 'pity for France' was indeed true patriotism by her definition.

The same cult of greatness which falsified history had, however, in her view, polluted all other forms of cultural activity. In the arts, for example, she sees the pursuit of greatness to be a submission to social pressure, and a distancing of art from goodness which is its true destiny. Genius, as we have seen, is a matter of paying attention to ideal good, and art of genius is only the incarnation of that ideal good in beauty. Since its other manifestations are truth and justice, there is a mysterious unity between all these incarnations of goodness, and an artist of genius therefore possesses a kind of sainthood. Simone Weil's startling but entirely logical conclusion therefore is that where there is a work of genius there is also saintliness; the contemplation of absolute goodness which produces beauty in art also produces, necessarily, purity in living. Her list of perfect purity in French literature is not long: among poets it includes Villon, the Renaissance poets Maurice Scève, d'Aubigné and Théophile de Viau, Racine (when he wrote *Phèdre*), Lamartine, Vigny and Gérard de Nerval (although with reservations), and Mallarmé. In prose she claims only Rabelais, Montaigne (but notably through the influence of his friend, La Boétie), Descartes (although elsewhere he is criticised for deliberately obscuring scientific results so that no one could 'steal' them from him), Retz, Molière, Montesquieu and Rousseau. It is clearly not difficult to claim a fair amount of genius in the work of all these writers; sanctity, however, is another matter for some of them at least, if it bears any relationship at all to normal codes of morality. Rousseau's well-known inability to take notice of the real people who were his responsibility, because he was preoccupied with wider speculations, surely goes not only against such codes, but against the definitions of justice laid down by Simone Weil herself. There seems to be a certain tautology involved in her categorisation of works of genius and their authors: because goodness is one and indivisible, beauty and sanctity necessarily go together, and one does not need to examine the life of an artist to know whether it was saintly or not: his work is sufficient for us to deduce this.

Turning from the artistic to the intellectual world, Simone Weil sees in the development of modern science another illustration of the aspiration to false greatness, and therefore a principle of *déracinement*. Her main criticism of modern science relates to the motives of scientists themselves. She sets out to show that the only genuine motive for scientific research is the love of truth, and that this is the one thing modern scientists do not on the whole possess. Truth is an aspect of absolute goodness, and the only appropriate attitude to absolute goodness is loving attention; scientists, on the other hand, are concerned with the acquisition of knowledge, and knowledge cannot be an object of love. She claims in fact that truth itself cannot be an object of love either, since it cannot be an object at all; it is rather reality itself which should be the object of the scientist's love:

> To desire truth is to desire a direct contact with reality. To desire a contact with reality is to love it. One only desires truth in order to love in truth. One desires to know the truth about what one loves. Instead of speaking of love of truth, it would be better to speak of a spirit of truth in love.[8]

But scientists since the Renaissance have put themselves outside the love of truth by releasing themselves from the realm of good and evil. Science studies only the facts, and facts, force, matter, considered in themselves, are not lovable.

What then has replaced this love as a motive for science? she asks. First of all, there are the technical applications of science, or rather, the prestige the scientist derives from them through feeling himself to be part of something great. But again, it is false greatness, greatness independent of all goodness. It is, however, almost the only aspect of science that interests the public, and without it a great number of scientists would not feel the profession to be worth their while. The problem with technical applications is that success alone counts, and not the relationship of the application to good and evil. Thus a scientist on the brink of an earth-shattering discovery is unlikely to hold back because the application of his discovery will do more harm than good (E 217). (In fact, there have been a few instances of this in recent years, but it does not seem that Simone Weil had heard of any in her own times.) She contrasts here, as on other points relating to science, the attitude of the Greeks towards technology. If the Greeks remained at a fairly early stage of technical development, she says, it was not because their science was not capable of such development, but because their scientists had no interest in it.

They were wary of technical inventions which could be put to use by tyrants and conquerers, so much so that instead of offering to the public the greatest number of technical discoveries and selling them to the highest bidder, they kept rigorously secret those discoveries they came across more or less by accident (*E* 208).

Other motives for the work of the modern scientist are obvious, and Simone Weil enumerates some of them. A sense of professional duty is one; scientists are paid to 'produce science' ('fabriquer de la science'), and so they produce it. Honour and recognition of all kinds, professional advancement, reputation, the esteem of colleagues, all are important motives. Because scientists in the end talk only to scientists, they act and react on a collective level most of the time. Since most scientific research depends on team-work, any theory refused by the collective 'village' is still-born, and has no chance of making its way. Simone Weil identifies a kind of Darwinian survival of the fittest at work in science, where theories grow as if by chance (*E* 219). Like any other product of the collective, it is subject also to fashion.

The spirit of truth is thus entirely lacking from science, as from other manifestations of the human spirit. 'The atrocious ills with which we are struggling at present [. . .] come entirely from that source' (*E* 221), she claims, setting the blame for the uprooting of Europe fairly and squarely at the door of untruth. The only way in which the spirit of truth can once more be incarnated in science is for the scientist to be motivated by love of the object which is the material of his study. 'That object is the universe in which we live' (*E* 221), and what is lovable in it is its beauty. 'The true definition of science is that it is the study of the beauty of the world.'[9] Simone Weil comes full circle, picking up the relationship of science with the good with which she opened her remarks on science, when she observes: 'The scientist has for his aim the union of his own mind with that mysterious wisdom eternally inscribed in the universe. How then could there be opposition or even separation between the spirit of science and that of religion? Scientific investigation is only one form of religious contemplation'.[10]

It is clear from this how far science had deviated from what Simone Weil considers to be its true role. The Great Beast in the form of collective values had taken over, as it tended to in all other forms of cultural and social organisation. To remedy this and to create a form of social life in which people could feel genuinely rooted, it is necessary to foster the impersonal in the human being; in fact, 'the relationships between the collectivity and the individual should be established with the sole object of setting aside all that prevents the growth and the mysterious germination of the impersonal part of the soul'.[11] It is important to take account of Simone Weil's vocabulary here; the impersonal is not the anonymous: that is rather a feature of the collective, which submerges the individual and prevents its proper development, and it is that which is only too much in evidence in modern society. The impersonal for Simone Weil is, on the contrary, the only thing that is sacred in a human being, because it is the manifestation of that person's relationship with absolute goodness. Because that relationship can exist only through loving attention, the impersonal for Simone Weil is full of joy, warmth, beauty. It is this which one is to seek to foster in society, and clearly, on these terms, nothing could be more positive or, unhappily, further from existing reality, as she herself admits (*EL* 21).

She does, however, have precise suggestions for reform, some contained in *L'Enracinement*, some in the other 'London essays', all related to the particular situation of Europe at war, but reaching far beyond the wartime situation. One of the questions she considered was that of the legitimacy of government: clearly this posed particular difficulties for France at the time; many Frenchmen indeed refused to recognise the legitimacy of de Gaulle as leader of the nation, not necessarily because they supported Pétain with any particular enthusiasm, but rather because de Gaulle was not a legally elected leader and thus offended democratic principle. In an essay on the legitimacy of the Provisional Government in London, Simone Weil set out to show that de Gaulle was not in fact a usurper. Interest in the legitimacy of the government had disappeared from the French mentality long before war broke out. In July 1940 the end of the Third Republic had caused scarcely a murmur of regret or concern, and few had appeared interested in what was to replace it. Far from having been the victim of theft, the French people had simply let the treasure of legitimate government fall out of their hands and had not even bothered to look down to see where it fell. In these circumstances, de Gaulle had picked up the treasure, and announced that he would hold it in safe keeping until the owner was in a fit state to claim it back (*EL* 61). The very flexible but entirely clear definition she gives of legitimacy in another essay could apply with no problem to de Gaulle's wartime regime: 'Legitimacy is constituted by the free consent of the people to the totality of the authorities to which it is subject'.[12]

As a general rule, legitimacy exists when those that govern are guided by concern for justice and public good, when the governed are confident that this is so and that this state of affairs is likely to continue, and when the leaders desire power only so long as the people retain this confidence (*EL* 66). A political regime based on legitimacy is composed of a double mechanism, the first aspect of which ensures attachment to legitimacy on the part of those who hold power, the second providing penalties for those who offend against the principle of legitimacy. In a parliamentary regime, elections correspond to the first aspect, the possibility of being thrown out of power the second. But in Simone Weil's view these mechanisms had no longer been functioning properly in France for a long time before its fall in 1940. Elections had become a sinister farce, and the use of commercial advertising had reduced election campaigns to a kind of prostitution. In addition, the functions of parliamentarian, minister etc. had become as it were professions, where the number of professionals available was not significantly greater than the number of places to fill. The penal mechanism therefore no longer operated.

Even if it had, Simone Weil tended to feel that it was not adequate to meet the scale of abuse possible. We have seen how she insisted that responsibility should be in direct proportion to power, so that punishment of those in authority for abuses committed should be related very directly to their potential for causing harm. In the case of the Provisional Government, Simone Weil suggests the following controls: de Gaulle should be allowed to continue to function as head of government, but should submit all his acts and those of other members of his government to a special tribunal, who would be empowered to judge and punish if necessary with the death penalty, in accordance with a new Declaration which would fulfil the function which the 1789 Declaration of Human Rights had always been powerless to fulfil, and on which de Gaulle would swear a solemn oath. In order that this mechanism should function properly, de Gaulle should renounce any idea of a future political career, and prevent the constitution of any group of his followers which might exert undesirable pressure (*EL* 70–1).

Simone Weil's double fear in connection with the workings of society, fear of the mechanisms of force and fear of the collective, is evident here. If her measures seem harsh in the context of political activity as it operates, it is because she had such an acute grasp of those forces which destroy the free development of the individual in society. The same remarks must apply to her condemnation of political parties. It is true that her main targets are continental European political parties; she had a good deal of admiration for the British bi-party system as it then operated. Political parties as they existed in France she felt to be an almost unmitigated evil, for three main reasons: firstly, a political party is a machine for producing collective passion. Secondly, a political party is an organisation designed to exercise collective pressure on the minds of its members, and this can only obscure truth. Thirdly, the sole aim of a political party is its own limitless growth. It is by nature totalitarian; it is like an animal being fattened up, for which process alone the universe exists (*EL* 135). Above all, it prevents the free exercise of the individual intelligence in its search for justice and the public good. The need to adhere to the party line takes precedence over judgement, even though a party, being a collectivity, cannot think, and therefore cannot be said to have a doctrine. Simone Weil's absolute and uncompromising regard for the truth made it impossible for her to submit to any grouping which claimed to think for her. We have already seen her stance with regard to the church, which she rejected for essentially similar reasons. 'If one recognises that there is one truth, then one is only allowed to think what is true. One then thinks something, not because one is French, or Catholic, or Socialist, but because the irresistible light of the obvious obliges one to think thus and not otherwise'.[13]

What, then, does Simone Weil envisage to replace political parties? Certainly not a single party, which she describes as the highest degree of evil. What she wants is a much clearer distinction of the function of various groupings, and greater control over what they do. She would allow groupings based on common interest — trade unions, for instance, to defend the interests of working people. Such groupings, however, would be subject to clear limits, and must in no way be allowed to restrict ideas. In any milieu where ideas were a subject for discussion, a kind of perpetual to-and-fro must operate; recruitment to any such grouping would be by simple affinity, and members would be free to come and go and express opinions as they wished. Free communication of ideas would be a proof that the group was operating as it should, and too great a uniformity of ideas would render it suspect. Above all, nothing resembling excommunication should exist, or indeed any form of discipline for divergence of thought. Simone Weil seems to have inherited Rousseau's belief in the way people unite in reason and diverge in passion, so that where they agree it is likely to be in the public interest, whereas disagreement is indicative of individual passion (*EL* 128). She admits that this reasoning breaks down, however, as soon as collective passion operates, since passion when it is collective is far more dangerous than any individual. Hence her dislike of political parties, as creators of collective passion.

There is clearly much to admire both in Simone Weil's criticisms of the way the party system operated in her time, and in her suggestions for reform, while it is permissible to have doubts as to the practical implications of their implementation. She herself indeed saw many of the problems involved, but seems to have felt that in a desperate situation such as she interpreted it, desperate measures were essential. She also considered, however, that at one or two rare moments in history a genuinely free society had existed, one which had nourished the individual's need for roots and allowed his free development. One such was the Languedoc civilisation of the twelfth century, the civilisation of the Troubadours, which also gave rise to the Cathar heresy which was persecuted and finally annihilated by the Church. Simone Weil had an intense admiration for this civilisation, which she considered to be one of the few in history which had refused force, and while in Marseilles wrote two articles on it for the *Cahiers du Sud*. Her admiration for the doctrine of the Cathars sprang in large measure from the fact that it was a living religion and not simply a philosophy. In her view, 'around Toulouse in the twelfth century the most elevated thought existed in a human milieu and not simply in the minds of a certain number of individuals'.[14] This was possible because the Languedoc civilisation was religious in its inspiration, based on a refusal of force and collective values. According to her, it was a model of order, freedom and harmony between social classes. She notes the joyfulness that seems to radiate from what we know of it, and the free circulation of ideas which meant that persecution of difference simply did not exist. Even under pressure from the Crusades against the Cathars, this group was never ostracised, and Catholics too, although their Church was the source of the distress of the Languedoc, were treated with respect. On the part of the citizens of the Languedoc, the Crusades were undertaken much more out of patriotism than doctrinal partisanship. Relationships between individuals followed the same pattern of respect: hierarchy was never identified with a master–slave relationship, and obedience was not a source of humiliation. Respect was mutual, so that, for instance, the Count of Toulouse would consult the citizens before undertaking an important action. Altogether, the Languedoc civilisation was a model for Simone Weil of a society with roots which nourished its members instead of stifling them. But its spiritual strength, namely, its refusal of force, was its downfall in historical terms. Such a civilisation could never be a match for the crusading might of the medieval Church, and it perished through its own virtue.

Interesting additional light is thrown on this civilisation and on Simone Weil's ideas on the positive role which a well-ordered society can fulfil, by her play, *Venise sauvée*, which she began in 1940 and worked on intermittently, leaving it unfinished, however, at her death. It is based on the Abbé de Saint-Réal's narrative of the plot against Venice by the Spanish empire, but Simone Weil changes aspects of the spirit of the narrative to fit her dual conception of society. Spain represents for her the totalitarian Great Beast wishing to devour the flourishing city of Venice, simply because it existed outside the Empire. The notes Simone Weil made for the play indicate clearly that she took as her model here the Roman Empire: 'In the 1st Act, idea of Empire./Social element without roots, the social without the idea of city, Roman Empire./A Roman always thought *we*'.[15] She wanted at the same time, however, to give an idea of the inevitability of the attack, and she outlines all the valid political reasons for absorbing Venice into the Empire. The mercenaries who are leading the attack are characterised as 'uprooted' exiles who hate the Venetians for having roots. The policy is to destroy as much of the past in its tangible form of buildings, art treasures etc. as possible, so that the Venetians in their turn will be uprooted. Only then will they submit to being enslaved. Venice itself is defined as 'a city./City, that term does not conjure up the social element./Being rooted is something different from the social element'.[16] Venice represents a contact with nature, the past, tradition; it is a mediator, that is to say an earthly phenomenon which allows human attention to pass upwards towards absolute good, rather than itself becoming an object of idolatry, a means rather than an end. It is nourishment for its citizens, a unique substance which, once destroyed, can never be replaced (*E* 13).

Like the Languedoc civilisation, Venice has no weapons of force to fend off attack from a totalitarian power. Venice is saved, however, saved by its beauty. In Simone Weil's version, one of the adventurers who has been elected to lead the invasion party, Jaffier, suddenly loses heart when he sees the beauty of Venice and realises all that will be destroyed by the venture. He betrays the plot and the attack is foiled. For Simone Weil this represents a moment of supernatural intuition on the part of Jaffier. The beauty of Venice makes him perceive its reality, and he suddenly sees the venture in relationship with absolute goodness. No other motive would have sufficed to save the city, since 'naturally', according to the laws of force, the conspiracy would have gone ahead.

One of the main themes here, as in Simone Weil's interpretation of the destroyed Languedoc civilisation, is obviously that of the vulnerability of purity, beauty, goodness. She compares their destruction to the 'fall of fruit-tree blossom. To know that what is most precious is not rooted in existence. That is beautiful'.[17] Indeed, the fact that a civilisation has been destroyed becomes on occasion almost a criterion for judging its purity: success and longevity in cultural terms almost necessarily involve some kind of pact with the collective devil.

Another point which must be emphasised in Simone Weil's consideration of society in its positive potential is the great stress she laid on the past. A civilisation whose past has been destroyed or adulterated, usually through conquest but sometimes through neglect, is as good as dead. Any reform in society must take account of the past, must always appear to be either a return to a past which has been allowed to decay, or the adaptation of an institution to new conditions. The object of such an adaptation is then not a change, but the maintenance of an invariable relationship. Using a mathematical illustration, she points out that in the relationship 12/4, if 4 becomes 5, the relationship is maintained by making 12 into 15, and not by retaining the 12. There is in her, as we have already seen, a systematic refusal of revolution which combines in exhilarating fashion with a desire to leave no idea untested, and a radical rejection of much that twentieth-century society stands for.

A final observation should perhaps be made here. What makes some of Simone Weil's proposals seem unreal in practice is their application to the modern all-pervasive State system. Many of them can be seen in a totally different light when applied on a smaller scale. Often she seems to be harking back to the Greek city-state, or the medieval corporations: at the same time, she was certainly one of the first of the modern thinkers to realise that 'small is beautiful'. The same remarks can be applied to her thinking on reform in the world of work, to which I wish to turn next. An appraisal of that area of her thinking should enable us to judge better whether hers is simply a wilful retreat from the present into a past Golden Age, or whether her sharp perception that society has somewhere taken a wrong turning can be justified.

Notes

1. These essays consisted of papers written for the Free French services for whom she was working, and were destined for circulation among her colleagues. The majority remained unpublished until their appearance in the *Ecrits de Londres et dernières lettres* in 1957, although a few appeared in *La Table Ronde* and in *Preuves* in the 1950s.
2. *E* 9: 'La notion d'obligation prime celle de droit, qui lui est subordonnée et relative'.
3. *EL* 78: 'Quiconque a son attention et son amour tournés en fait vers la réalité étrangère au monde reconnaît en même temps qu'il est tenu, dans la vie publique et privée, par l'unique et perpétuelle obligation de remédier, dans l'ordre de ses responsabilités et dans la

mesure de son pouvoir, à toutes les privations de l'âme et du corps susceptibles de détruire ou de mutiler la vie terrestre d'un être humain quel qu'il soit'.
4. *E* 11: 'La conscience humaine n'a jamais varié sur ce point. Il y a des milliers d'années, les Egyptiens pensaient qu'une âme ne peut pas être justifiée après la mort si elle ne peut pas dire: "Je n'ai laissé personne souffrir de la faim"'.
5. *EL* 40: '[Le châtiment est uniquement un procédé] pour fournir du bien pur à des hommes qui ne le désirent pas; l'art de punir est l'art d'éveiller chez les criminels le désir du bien pur par la douleur ou même par la mort'.
6. *E* 45: 'Un être humain a une racine par sa participation réelle, active et naturelle à l'existence d'une collectivité qui conserve vivants certains trésors du passé et certains pressentiments d'avenir. . . . Chaque être humain a besoin d'avoir de multiples racines. Il a besoin de recevoir la presque totalité de sa vie morale, intellectuelle, spirituelle, par l'intermédiaire des milieux dont il fait naturellement partie'.
7. *EL* 54: '[Une chose] à aimer non pour sa gloire, son prestige, son éclat, ses conquêtes, son rayonnement, son expansion future, mais en elle-même, dans sa nudité et sa réalité . . .'.
8. *E* 215: 'Désirer la vérité, c'est désirer un contact direct avec la réalité. Désirer un contact avec une réalité, c'est l'aimer. On ne désire la vérité que pour aimer dans la vérité. On désire connaître la vérité de ce qu'on aime. Au lieu de parler d'amour de la vérité, il vaut mieux parler d'un esprit de vérité dans l'amour'.
9. *E* 222: 'La vraie définition de la science, c'est qu'elle est l'étude de la beauté du monde'.
10. Ibid.: 'Le savant a pour fin l'union de son propre esprit avec la sagesse mystérieuse éternellement inscrite dans l'univers. Dès lors comment y aurait-il opposition ou même séparation entre l'esprit de la science et celui de la religion? L'investigation scientifique n'est qu'une forme de la contemplation religieuse'.
11. *EL* 21: 'Les rapports entre la collectivité et la personne doivent être établis avec l'unique objet d'écarter ce qui est susceptible d'empêcher la croissance et la germination mystérieuse de la partie impersonnelle de l'âme'.
12. *EL* 92: 'La légitimité est constituée par le libre consentement du peuple à l'ensemble des autorités auxquelles il est soumis'. It is worth noting that Renan, in the nineteenth century, had held a similar notion.
13. *EL* 137: 'Si on reconnaît qu'il y a une vérité, il n'est permis de penser que ce qui est vrai. On pense alors telle chose, non parce qu'on se trouve être en fait Français, ou catholique, ou socialiste, mais parce que la lumière irrésistible de l'évidence oblige à penser ainsi et non autrement'.
14. *PSO* 65: 'Autour de Toulouse au XIIe siècle la plus haute pensée

vivait dans un milieu humain et non pas seulement dans l'esprit d'un certain nombre d'individus'.
15. *C*2 206; *P* 44: 'Dans le 1er acte, idée de l'*Empire./Social sans racines, social sans cité: empire romain.*/Un Romain pensait toujours *nous*' (Simone Weil's italics).
16. Ibid.: '[Venise est] une cité./Cité, cela n'évoque pas du social./L'enracinement est autre chose que le social'.
17. *C*2 172: 'Chute des pétales d'arbres fruitiers en fleur. Savoir que le plus précieux n'est pas enraciné dans l'existence. Cela est beau'.

4 The Theory and Practice of Work

A meditation on the theory and practice of work, and a desire to experience manual work at first hand in as many of its forms as possible, provide a constant in the development of Simone Weil's philosophy. Even as a student, she realised the importance of work as a phenomenon central to the understanding of man's place in the universe, and the various essays which have been preserved from this time show her beginning to distinguish herself from Alain's teaching precisely in the depth of her thinking on the world of work, while the very last words of *L'Enracinement*, possibly the last she ever wrote, are on the same subject. This need to experience manual work at first hand was the motivating force for one of her most fruitful experiences, that of the months she spent as a factory-hand. So great was the importance she gave to a right attitude to work that she considered that the notion of work as a human value was probably the only contribution that could be said to have been made to civilisation by the modern world, just as the lack of such a notion was the only thing that Ancient Greece could be reproached with (*OL* 140). In the essay 'Réflexions sur les causes de la liberté et de l'oppression sociale' written before her factory experiences, she is clear that 'the most fully human civilisation would be one which had manual work at its centre' (*OL* 137), whereas at the end of *L'Enracinement* she declares that it is easy to define the place of manual work in a well-ordered society: 'it ought to be its spiritual centre' (*E* 256).

We have already seen how Simone Weil considered that truly free action occurs when every gesture arises out of thought initiated by the person performing the gesture. In her early writings, as at the end of her life, this idea is linked to its corollary: thought is valid only when realised in action. Thoughts which do not have to pass the test of necessity can have no reality, as she points out in the early *Leçons de philosophie* dating from her year in Roanne. Philosophy itself exists exclusively in action and practice, according to a note in *La Connaissance surnaturelle* (*CS* 335), claiming that 'for the man living in this world, here below, tangible matter — inert matter and flesh — is the filter, the screen, the universal criterion of what is real in thought; the domain of thought in its entirety, nothing excepted. Matter is our infallible judge'.[1] It is precisely because of this that the manual worker is in fact in a position of great privilege, or would be in a civilisation where manual work was properly conceived, since he or she is obliged daily to put thought into action. A manual worker in the act of working cannot entertain unreal thought, because the demands of the task he is performing constantly bring him face to face with reality. He is at grips with 'naked necessity', as Simone Weil puts it, dependent only on himself. In an ideal situation, he is subject to necessity and not to force, and his mind is free therefore to create relationships, grasp notions of time concerning the passage from one moment to the next, the prediction of future actions, etc.

I shall return to Simone Weil's ideas on what constitutes a proper attitude to manual work. From the few examples above, however, it is clear that the relationship between thought and work is the crucial one for her. All her criticisms of the industrial process, and all her suggestions for reform, revolve around the central idea that, for a variety of reasons, in the modern world thought has been divorced from action. In her later writings, this is expressed in terms of *déracinement* ('uprootedness'), while her earlier essays tend to analyse it in Marxist terms, as the division of labour into manual and intellectual, although her observations remain as happily free of Marxist jargon as of any other. In these essays she is mainly concerned with industrial work: although she was interested in agricultural labour from an early stage, an analysis of rural conditions has to wait until the war years.

In the dissertation which she wrote for her diploma in philosophy, Simone Weil traces the way in which the former domination of the people by the priests has given way in modern times to that of working people by intellectuals, of those that do by those that know. This domination was a central preoccupation from her student days onwards: as we saw, if she participated in evening classes for working people it was essentially in order to liberate them from the overpowering influence of intellectuals like herself. In this dissertation she traces the way in which ordinary people have always accepted the mystification of what is seen as a higher force, but which in reality enslaves them, by depriving them of the ability to take control mentally of what they are doing. In the 'Réflexions sur les causes de la liberté et de l'oppression sociale', she underlines the need to give back to working people the power of mind over matter, a form of material life where physical effort would be directed exclusively by clear thought, so that every worker had to control not only the adaptation of his efforts to the work to be accomplished, but also the coordination of his efforts with those of everyone else (*OL* 131).

One crucial way in which working people have been deprived of this capacity, according to Simone Weil, is in a mutilation of their sense of time. The early essays show her very conscious of the importance of a right perception of time in the interpretation of the universe in general. In the essay entitiled 'Du temps' ('Concerning Time'),[2] she defines work as that indirect action by which I act upon myself and upon the world, indirect because subject to time, which intervenes between the present state of things and any future state I may envisage. Potentially, work is thus the conquest of time. But the modern industrial worker is deprived of this capacity to enter into a real relationship with time in several important ways, which form the basis of Simone Weil's analysis of the industrial process, as well as subtending many of her comments on her own factory experience.

One of the features of the modern factory which she found the most mutilating was that of 'rationalisation', or 'Taylorisation', the study of working practices with a view to getting maximum production out of the employees. She sees it as a new departure in the approach to scientific method: previously science had been applied to the use of the forces of nature, whereas now it is turned on the human workforce (*CO* 215). But attention is only directed towards them in the interests of production, and the application of Taylor's methods to the factory results in an inevitable clash of interests, a clash in which the worker is the loser. A factory is for turning out objects in as great a number and as cheaply as possible, and factory employees are there to assist the machines in that process. However, these same employees have needs and aspirations which frequently do not coincide with those of the needs of production. Hence the conflict (*CO* 218). In order to produce ever more objects, the worker is obliged to go ever faster; one of the features that most distressed Simone Weil in her own factory experience was precisely the inhuman rhythm she was supposed to adopt. Human beings are so constituted as to need a moment of reflection between actions, and the frenetic pace of work necessary to survive materially under the system precluded any such reflection.

Piece-work was inevitably another target for her condemnation, at least in the way in which she saw it operated. It is a feature of rationalisation, in so far as it enables an individual industrial worker as part of a team to produce more parts, since he is not obliged to change process, move around the factory, and so forth, in order to complete a manufactured article. But to Simone Weil it could never be made acceptable, since it destroyed in the worker the sense of the whole in which he was involved. Frequently, she observes, the worker has no idea what part he plays in the industrial process, or even what object he is helping to produce. He is fixed eternally in a present moment, and cannot foresee where the part he is making will be going next. His only obligation is to go faster and still faster, threatened with hunger if he does not keep up the rhythm imposed from the outside.

It is thus in part that Simone Weil explains a worker's resentment when directed to change job within the factory. Any break in the rhythm means a diminution in take-home pay. But there is also a factor which concerns the worker's perception of time. Orders are given abruptly, without any explanation, and the worker is thus made to feel that his time is entirely at someone else's disposal. If on the contrary the change was prepared in advance, he would be able to grasp and organise the future, even while still being obliged to obey. Simone Weil knew, however, that obedience in the system meant humiliation; consequently the worker could not envisage change in the future without passing through humiliation. The future entailed either that, or an endless repetition of the same process, which meant that it was impossible to contemplate. Thought thus retreated into the present moment (*CO* 245), creating a sort of stupor in the mind. In the letters she wrote to the factory manager, Auguste Detœuf, Simone Weil outlines the conditions for free obedience. She points out that she is not naturally insubordinate: she has only contempt for someone who does not know how to obey. But she cannot accept those forms of subordination 'where intelligence, ingenuity, will, professional conscience play a part only in the elaboration of orders given by the foreman, and where the execution of those orders demands only passive submission in which neither the mind nor the heart have any part; so that the subordinate plays the role more or less of an object manipulated by someone else's intelligence'.[3]

The idea of being an object manipulated by an exterior will picks up in a striking way Simone Weil's condemnation of slavery, as for example in her essay *L'Iliade* ou le poème de la force' (referred to in Part I above), where force makes human beings into slaves, that is to say, inanimate objects. The power of decision-making, of organising his time according to the perceptions of his own intelligence, is denied the worker as it is denied the slave, and they are both reduced to the status of a mere thing (*OL* 116). As Simone Weil notes, in the factory the products of the industrial process are given a higher status than that of the people who operate the machines that manufacture them. Again, the question of time in relation to the future is important: a slave is a person who can look to no reward for his labours other than that of the maintenance of the status quo (*C3* 183). Likewise, an industrial worker works in order to eat, and eats only so that he can go back to work again the next day. The status of slave is emphasised by the fact that the worker has no automatic right of citizenship in the factory: he is tolerated while he is useful, and laid off without explanation as soon as he can be dispensed with. She gives a vivid description in her factory journal of women waiting at an open factory gate in the pouring rain on a winter's morning, knowing that they had no right to enter until the siren went, and notes the humiliation of clocking on at a mechanically determined moment, neither a minute early nor late, which has nothing to do with the needs of the individual worker.

It has sometimes been argued that Simone Weil was abnormally, even morbidly sensitive to the necessarily abrasive nature of relationships within the factory, and that her criticisms simply reveal her bourgeois susceptibilitites, since ordinary working people used to the discipline of the factory did not complain in the same way. It is true, obviously, that most people simply get on with life and, if they are not given any reason to suppose things can change, complain very little. But in a way this simply illustrates her point: she was able to perceive the way in which the worker's intelligence counted for nothing because she came from the outside, from a part of the system where intelligence was valued before all else, and therefore felt acutely the way in which hers was systematically destroyed within the factory. Ordinary factory workers, however, were obliged to accept the degree of abasement to which they found themselves reduced, precisely because the human spirit is conditioned to accept the unacceptable when it cannot effect change. In other contexts Simone Weil points out how difficult it is for an afflicted person to express his affliction, and how difficult it is to assist such a person, since he gives every sign not of wanting to change his situation, but, on the contrary, of wanting to justify it. One of the things that most struck her in her own factory experience was the way in which oppression generated submission, to the point where she herself, in the few short months of factory work, lost all inclination to contest an order or to retaliate in any way. It is probably true that a large number of slaves in the heyday of the nineteenth-century slave-trade would have been reluctant to change their status, but this cannot be used to justify the institution of slavery. Even when working people start making demands, Simone Weil believes, it would be wrong to take them literally: these demands are only the sign of their suffering, and should be interpreted thus (E 53).

The chief evil in the factory system for Simone Weil is therefore the way in which it deprives the worker of the use of his intelligence, and all the reforms she suggests have the need to restore the balance between manual and intellectual work as their main motivation. This restoration has not even been attempted, she feels, because the would-be reformers have always concentrated on the wrong things, and the working classes have been led astray with false solutions to their predicament. The measures proposed are always of a judicial nature, and never get to the heart of the problem(E 53). One of these, that proposed by Marx, is revolution, and we have already seen Simone Weil's deep reservations concerning change by this means. She remained convinced that reversing the relationship between oppressed and oppressors would result, not in the reign of justice and equality, but in a new oppression; in that, the events of the twentieth century have largely borne her out.

Another false solution identified by Simone Weil and designed to relieve the worker's situation, one which has lost none of its prestige, is that of money. She gives a shrewd analysis of the psychological hold that money has over people who do not have enough for even their minimum requirements. Oppressed as they are by fatigue and the daily treadmill of simple existence, which prevents them paying attention to their situation, they welcome what she calls 'the clarity of figures' when someone begins to talk to them about wage-increases (*EL* 23). In her criticism of the use of figures to mesmerise the population, Simone Weil comes out strongly against the whole modern western tendency to think a solution to a problem has been found when once it has been quantified, but also against the debasing effect of using money as an intermediary in all relationships. Not only does money not provide a solution to the problems of industrial workers, it debases work itself by becoming the sole motive for effort. It is in this way that the workers' movement, including its trade unions, its parties and its left-wing intellectuals, has betrayed the working class, by bargaining about figures when they should be talking about nothing other than the souls of working people (ibid.). By 'soul' here, she clearly means that part of a human being that has needs other than the simply material, the satisfaction of which leads to that genuine *enracinement* which we considered in the previous chapter.

What does Simone Weil herself propose, then, to replace both the oppression and the false solutions being put forward? Firstly, she is very clear that there is in manual work an inevitable element of suffering and hardship, and no amount of reform will ever change that. Freedom in work is thus defined by a submission to necessity, and not to force, in other words by a free acceptance of the hardships and freedom from arbitrary and incomprehensible orders. She points out that any suffering is easier to accept if one understands the necessary factors that have caused it (*CO* 139). As she writes to Detœuf: 'The acceptance of those physical and moral sufferings that are inevitable, in the precise degree to which they are inevitable, is the only way of preserving one's dignity. But acceptance and submission are two quite different things'.[4] In this way, she recognises that monotony and boredom are part of human existence, and in certain circumstances have to be accepted. They can in any case be extremely beautiful as an image of the human condition: as she points out, there is more monotony in Gregorian chant or a Bach concerto than in an operetta (*CO* 256). But the human mind is made to dominate time, and for this must have both uniformity and variety in a mixture that is comprehensible.

To render the whole process comprehensible is her ultimate aim. A first step, she suggests in one of the essays on her factory experience, would be a genuine effort at workers' education within the factory itself. The production workers should, for example, be shown around the factory at intervals, the time thus spent being paid at the normal rate, and given technical explanations of the processes involved. Even better, their families should be invited to do the same: is it not grotesque that a woman should never see the place where her husband gives the best of himself all day, every day (*CO* 254)? Also, from time to time, workers should be shown the object which they have had a part in making. Ultimately, however, the very system by which they spend their day repeating a few mechanical gestures as part of a greater whole should disappear: Simone Weil envisages the creation of what she calls 'multi-purpose automatic machines', which would give the operative a much greater responsibility in the manufacture of the desired object. She clearly foresees increased mechanisation, beyond the technical possibilities of the time she was writing. What she did not foresee, of course, any more than others at the time, were the social consequences of the resulting vastly reduced workforce.

In all this she envisages a much greater worker participation in decision-making, and here she predicts the various movements of worker-control that have arisen since the war. The letters to Detœuf reveal her disappointment that he found unacceptable her canvassing the opinions of workers on the work they were doing. She would like to see an exchange of views on a basis of complete equality between workers and bosses, not just so that the latter would understand better the grievances of the former, but so that the former would understand the constraints under which the latter operated. If in the course of such an exchange, it became apparent that the ignorance of the workforce was a major obstacle to the creation of a more humane system, then a series of articles in the factory journal with a deliberately popular appeal could provide the answer.

Her suggestions here are practical and positive, and, indeed, so much of what she proposes is taken for granted these days that it is hard to remember just how absolute was the division between management and workforce at the time she was writing, and to understand why her apparently moderate proposals had such a negative reception. The image she gives in the essay 'Expérience de la vie d'usine' ('Experience of factory life') (*CO* 242), of what a modern factory could be, in contrast to what it actually was, has everything to please management, in so far as it is a vision of serious corporate effort towards a common goal. The harsh noise of metal on metal has a meaning, that of man's sustained and uninterrupted action on the world of objects. Even isolated by the noise, the individual has an almost intoxicating sense of being part of an active collectivity (a collectivity which in this context is acceptable to Simone Weil because each individual is exercising his mind and his will in an effort which transcends the individual, and to which he has consented).

Although clearly here Simone Weil is thinking of life in a large factory, on the whole her proposed reforms would abolish the huge and necessarily anonymous enterprise in favour of smaller units. Indeed, she suggests that where possible a worker could have his machine at home, organising his work as he thought fit. Such a machine would be given to a worker by the State, along with a house and a piece of land, upon marriage, provided he had successfully completed a series of technical tests designed to check his professional competence and general culture. A worker who did not pass the tests would continue with the status of wage-earner, but could at any time ask to do a course to improve his competence. The property thus acquired could not be transferred or disposed of in any way, but could be withrawn for professional incompetence. On the death of a worker (whom Simone Weil here assumes to be male), the property automatically passes back to the State, unless the widow were technically able to take over the job. Dependents would in any case be assured an equivalent standard of living.

Simone Weil seems to raise more problems than she solves here. She does not seem to be concerned, for example, at the increased possibility of exploitation by unscrupulous bosses or officials when the workforce is scattered in this way, as in the notorious abuse of out-workers in our own day. By making marriage a condition of property, she assumes its universal applicability, and casts women in the role of permanent dependents in a way that is not reflected in the particular concern she shows elsewhere in her writings for women workers as being, along with immigrant workers and the very young, among the most exploited in the factory. She is on safer ground when she proposes the creation of small workshop units to replace the large factory, and the increase in number of highly qualified professionals to replace the huge mass of unskilled workers who provided the main part of the workforce in her day. Her ideas for opening up the horizons of working people, by proper education programmes, adequate apprenticeships and cultural and technical visits to other parts of France paid for by industry, make good sense at least in their general inspiration, and reflect her constant belief in the intellectual capacities of ordinary people. They also make clear that *enracinement* in no way involves the narrowing of a worker's horizons.

Some of her ideas on the reform of the condition of agricultural workers bear a similar mark of unreality, at least in their practical application, to those noted above in respect of industrial workers. Others make good sense, especially when read in the context of her times. Where she is unreal, this is due partly to the fact that, in spite of her efforts to experience the peasant condition, and her instinctive understanding of certain aspects of it, she was never able to get as close to rural life as to urban conditions. Born and raised in Paris, she experienced the countryside as essentially something outside her immediate experience, and she was right to note also that the whole of the French educational system, in other words her whole intellectual frame of reference, was urban in its orientation. Also accurate is her perception of the way in which the rural inhabitant, and the peasant in particular, is despised by the town-dweller who thinks that if a peasant remains a peasant it is because he is too stupid to become anything else. Peasants have no power, no voice, and so they are ignored. Simone Weil's proposals for giving back dignity and therefore genuine rootedness to the peasant population include a complete reform of the education system, so that rural teachers would receive a different training from that of their urban counterparts. More emphasis should be put on the study of folklore and rural traditions in general, to give the rural inhabitant the feeling that he had a part to play in the development of human thought. Too often, Simone Weil notes, thought is presented as something exclusively urban in its origin, in which the peasant is tolerated as an outsider. But the peasant should not be excluded from science either: it should simply be presented differently. For industrial workers, science is dominated by mechanics, and can be understood thus by them, whereas the presentation of science in a rural context should revolve around the energy cycle by which solar energy descends into plants, where it is fixed by chlorophyll and concentrated in vegetable substance which is then consumed by people who gain from it energy with which to work the land.

When Simone Weil extends this purely scientific idea to the reading of Christian symbolism in rural life in general, one may have doubts as to its universal application to the modern world, although one should also remember that the essay in which she elaborates these ideas most fully, 'Le christianisme et la vie des champs' ('Christianity and rural life') (*PSO* 21–33), was written for Father Perrin in Marseilles, to be used therefore in a specifically Christian context. There is a sense, however, in which such a Christian reading of daily experience was for her self-evident, given that everyday material reality, properly interpreted, was a reflection of spiritual reality. She sets herself the task, therefore, of making manifest this reflection. 'It is a question of transforming, in as great a degree as possible, everyday life itself into a metaphor with divine meaning, into a parable.'[5] The Biblical parables serve as an obvious example of how such a transformation can be effected. For instance, she says, the peasant sowing seed can reflect on the parable of Christ as the sower and the death of the seed being a condition of new life, just as the death of carnal man is a condition of this rebirth spiritually. For a peasant sowing in this way, the hours spent working are as prayerful as those spent by a monk in his cell, without the work suffering in any way (*PSO* 24). The peasant, in fact, for Simone Weil, has a particularly privileged position (especially, one imagines, the French peasant), since by the energy he consumes he transforms his own flesh and blood into the bread and wine that are the end product of his work, just as Christ's flesh and blood were transformed.

Perhaps scepticism as regards Simone Weil's ideas on agricultural labour arises precisely because they seem to bear no relationship to modern farming methods. Whereas in industry she foresaw the development of new machines to take the heaviest burden off the operators manipulating them, in farming she never seems to have envisaged increased mechanisation. Given what we now know regarding factory farming and the over-mechanisation of farming methods, she may well have been right in her intuition that the small-scale, labour-intensive methods of the past were those ultimately able to restore dignity to those that work the land. But there is a profound reason for her unwillingness to envisage mechanisation: it would seem that, as far as she was concerned, manual labour on the land was a good in itself. It is clear that, viewed from her perspective, it is much more immediate in its contact with reality than factory work. The peasant grows food which he consumes, and which is immediately transformed into energy, whereas even Simone Weil recognised that the modern industrial worker had, at least to a large extent, to see his effort transformed into money, which he could then spend on food which someone else had grown. Furthermore, since the product of the peasant's work was more immediate, so were all his gestures. The reasons for his fatigue were more immediately obvious, and its spiritual significance easier to deduce.

In the last few pages of *L'Enracinement* in the section which begins 'Le travail physique consenti . . .' ('Manual work which is consented to . . .'), which was found among Simone Weil's papers after the first edition of *L'Enracinement* had appeared and added in subsequent impressions, Simone Weil brings out clearly what she considers to be that spiritual significance, and in some ways it applies more readily to work on the land than to factory work. It is an important text, and possibly her last word, literally, on the subject of manual work. It is also easy to misread: it has been taken, for instance, as an example of the intense pessimism of the last years of her life, a masochistic indulgence in the painful aspects of labour which is at odds with her earlier revolutionary ardour. It is in fact no such thing, although it is a text of great richness and complexity.

She begins with the arresting statement that consent to manual work is, after consent to death itself, the most perfect form of obedience (E 251). The idea of work as punishment, found in the story of the Fall in Genesis, has been misunderstood, she claims, because the idea of punishment itself has been distorted. We have already seen in the context of her social thought in general Simone Weil's views on punishment: far from being a means of excluding someone from the community, it was the only way of reintegrating them when a fault had been committed. This reintegration, however, could happen only if punishment were consented to. In the same way, man by sin has excluded himself from God's presence; God has ordained death on the one hand, and work on the other, as punishment, so that man might be reintegrated into spiritual communion with him. We have already touched on the idea of death in the context of Simone Weil's own end, and we will be returning to it, but for the moment it is important to note that manual work is almost the equivalent in spiritual potential to death itself. (This, of course, is one reason why she was so desperate for the reform of the industrial process, since the inhuman conditions operating in the factories destroyed a worker's soul before he had had an opportunity of consenting to its necessarily harsh aspects.) In these same few pages she makes the various trades and professions originate in a direct teaching by the gods in a past long since lost to human memory.

The value of physical labour lies in the fact that, unlike death, it is constantly present. Death is unreal unless the exact moment of its arrival is known, as in the case of the man condemned to death, so that most people do not perceive it in all its reality. Work, however, is a daily death, in so far as it consists in engaging one's whole being, soul and body, in the circuit of inert matter, making it become an intermediary between one state of matter and another. The movements of a worker's body, and the attention of his mind, are a function of the demands of the tool he is using, which itself is adapted to the material of the work in hand. Man is *not* merely inert matter, however, and it is in this that work is also a cause for suffering. Simone Weil claims, in a passage which returns to her old preoccupation with time, that it 'does violence to human nature' (E 255). The manual worker is subject to time, and therefore to reality, in a way that someone who works only with his mind is not: instead of being able to escape from time by allowing thought to fly freely back and forth, he is forced to experience time as duration, moment by moment, in the way that inert matter does. Work is governed by necessity, not by finality, in that people work in order to go on existing, whereas human desire urges them to aim at future goals, to want something they do not already possess (CO 261). Consent to the law that makes manual labour a necessary part of human existence is therefore an act of perfect obedience. Simone Weil is clear, however, that such consent is also a source of joy, because it is a contact with reality. Already in a note dating from 1933–4, she comments: 'work: to feel in the whole of oneself the existence of the world' (*C*1 18), and, on the same page, 'joy is nothing other than the feeling of reality'. The joy which we can experience in manual labour, when it is not rendered inhuman, is indeed the sign that it is a fundamental part of our nature, that such work is made for us (*C*1 16). How could it be otherwise, when work is defined as 'the original pact between man and nature, between soul and body' (*C*1 61)? To lower the status of manual work, by defiling it in the way that the modern factory does, is thus nothing less than sacrilege (*EL* 22).

It is impossible to overestimate the importance of the notion of manual work in Simone Weil's thought. It is in manual work that man fulfils his greatest potential, becomes most fully human, because it is there that all his faculties are most completely brought into play. It is therefore quite wrong to see in Simone Weil's approach some sort of self-immolation: she never varied in her conviction that work in which the mind had no part to play was a sacrilegious travesty of the real thing. An early note (also dating from 1933–4) demands that 'every act of work be accompanied by the knowledge of all the human effort (theoretical and technical) which has rendered and renders it possible',[6] while a passage in *L'Enracinement* stipulates: 'If on the one hand the whole spiritual life of the soul, on the other all knowledge concerning the material universe, are orientated towards the act of work, work occupies its true place in the thought of mankind. Instead of being a kind of prison, it is a contact with this world and the other'.[7]

In the light of such statements, Simone Weil's own motivation for wanting to experience the condition of the manual worker becomes clearer. It is not just a desire to identify with the dispossessed: if it is that too, it is because the working condition has been pitifully distorted away from its true destiny, and Simone Weil wanted first-hand knowledge of it in order to restore it to its true place. But her deepest motive sprang clearly from her conviction that only through manual work could she come into contact with the reality of the universe, in all its beauty and its implacability. Manual work, with its necessary part of pain and suffering, was the key to wisdom.

Notes

1. *CS* 336: 'Pour l'homme vivant en ce monde, ici-bas, la matière sensible — matière inerte et chair — est le filtre, le crible, le critère universel du réel dans la pensée; le domaine de la pensée tout entier, sans que rien soit excepté. La matière est notre juge infaillible'.
2. *Libres Propos* (Nîmes), 8, 20.8.29, pp. 387–92. No English translation available.
3. *CO* 151: '[Je ne puis accepter les formes de subordination] où l'intelligence, l'ingéniosité, la volonté, la conscience professionnelle n'ont à intervenir que dans l'élaboration des ordres par le chef, et où l'exécution exige seulement une soumission passive dans laquelle ni l'esprit ni le cœur n'ont part; de sorte que le subordonné joue presque le rôle d'une chose maniée par l'intelligence d'autrui'.
4. *CO* 145: 'L'acceptation des souffrances physiques et morales inévitables, dans la mesure précise où elles sont inévitables, c'est le seul moyen de conserver sa dignité. Mais acceptation et soumission sont deux choses bien différentes'.
5. *PSO* 24 'Il s'agit de transformer, dans la plus large mesure possible, la vie quotidienne elle-même en une métaphore à signification divine, en une parabole'.
6. *Cl* 84: 'que chaque acte du travail soit accompagné de la connaissance de tous les efforts humains (théoriques et techniques) qui l'ont rendu et qui le rendent possible'.
7. *E* 85: 'Si d'une part toute la vie spirituelle de l'âme, d'autre part toutes les connaissances scientifiques concernant l'univers matériel, sont orientées vers le travail, le travail tient sa juste place dans la pensée d'un homme. Au lieu d'être une espèce de prison, il est un contact avec ce monde et l'autre'.

5 The *Via Negativa*

There is no doubt that suffering in its various forms plays a crucial role in Simone Weil's philosophy. It is one of the aspects which causes the most problems to readers of Simone Weil, who sometimes have the uneasy feeling that there is a masochistic streak in her which invalidates the otherwise illuminating things she has to say, or at least renders them less universal in application. She certainly had more than a normal amount of contact with suffering in her short life. In personal terms she had to come to terms with it in the form of the headaches she suffered throughout adulthood. Her early contacts with Christianity were coloured by the realisation of the element of suffering at the heart of that religion — we have seen how it was the 'heart-rending sadness' of the processional songs of the Portuguese fisher-folk that so impressed her. If this was so, it was because they seemed to her to be expressing something fundamental about the human condition. Just prior to this, the suffering she had encountered during her months in the factory had broken her, physically and spiritually.

Clearly, the human condition itself involves necessarily a large part of suffering for every individual: we are born in pain, and many of us die in pain and distress also. But for Simone Weil there is more to it than this. We are born, according to her, in imperfection of a very particular kind, 'dans le mensonge', 'in a state of untruth', and any effort we make away from this state provokes suffering. Suffering is thus a part of the moral life, in so far as the knowledge sought is ultimately identified with goodness. Simone Weil often speaks of the 'taming' of the beast in us, the submission of the animal instincts to the 'superior' part of the soul which is orientated toward goodness.

If suffering is a necessary part of our existence, and of any progress in the order of goodness, Simone Weil is equally clear that it must not be sought for its own sake. In an early note she states firmly: 'I believe in the value of suffering to the extent that one does everything (that is honest) to avoid it'.[1] The parenthesis is revealing: the avoidance of suffering should never involve a lie. There is a remarkable note in the same notebook, where she sees her own life as full of joyful potential: 'Never forget that you have the whole world, the whole of life, in front of you . . . That, for you, life can and must be more real, fuller and more joyful than it has been perhaps for any human being . . . Do not mutilate it in advance by any renunciation. Do not allow it to be imprisoned by any affection'.[2] In her final letter to Maurice Schumann, she expresses the fear that in coming to London she has in fact followed some base instinct. 'For my nature is cowardly. Everything which is difficult and dangerous makes me afraid.'[3]

She strongly denies, therefore, that she has any natural taste for suffering, or any desire to provoke it. This important aspect of her both as a person and as a philosopher can be seen even more clearly in what she has to say on that very particular kind of suffering which she calls 'le malheur', affliction. Affliction, she says, is 'an uprooting of life, a more or less blunted equivalent of death itself, of which the soul is made irresistibly aware by the presence or apprehension of physical pain'.[4] Affliction is only present when the vital human forces are attacked in all their aspects, social, psychological and physical. The social aspect is essential: for affliction to be present there must be social degradation, or at least the apprehension of it. Physical pain is also essential, because if it is not present, the mind is free to escape in imagination away from its torment. Only physical pain has the power to nail us to the spot. It is significant that, once again, Simone Weil is concerned with the physical reality of the situation: for experience to be real it must pass the test of matter.

Between other forms of suffering and affliction there is at once continuity and a threshold. When once that threshold has been crossed the afflicted person enters a completely different world, cut off by his experience from that in which 'normal' people operate, so that there is mutual disregard and incomprehension. Simone Weil insists on the impossibility for a normally healthy person to contemplate affliction: affliction is ugly, it is grotesque, and the normal human reaction is to turn away, while at the same time blaming the afflicted for his affliction. The same inability to communicate seizes the afflicted person, who can neither express what he is suffering, nor ask for help to extricate himself from it. Nor are such people capable of extending compassion to others in the same situation: the loss of all sense of dignity, all sense of being, deprives the afflicted person of any feeling of having anything to offer. Affliction brands a person with 'that contempt, that disgust and even repulsion for oneself, that feeling of guilt and taint, which crime logically should produce and doesn't'.[5] It is, she says, the feeling of a total absence of goodness (*CS* 203).

It is clear that affliction is a condition so appalling that it cannot possibly be sought willingly by any human being. Simone Weil is quite clear on that point. In the letter to Schumann, she points out that, had she been seeking affliction as some kind of martrydom or self-gratification, in terms of her desire to participate adequately in the war-situation, it would have been easy for her to fall into enemy hands while still in France (*EL* 214). And yet there is a sense in which that statement must be qualified, and in fact she herself does so. Although affliction is defined 'by necessity', as something which one undergoes in spite of oneself, it can also be imposed 'by obligation'. Precisely because it is a condition impossible to accept, affliction can reveal reality in a way that nothing else can, and can therefore be seen in terms of vocation in a commitment to that reality. Affliction that has been truly consented to makes impossible the lies by which we make life bearable. Since there is nothing in affliction that a person can possibly desire, one can be sure that in that condition one is seeking nothing for oneself. The total absence of consolation in affliction is a guarantee of the absolute purity of the experience in the order of reality and illusion. Simone Weil's whole life was devoted to the pursuit of reality which she identifies with truth, and all the experiences she sought, often in spite of herself, have this truth as their ultimate goal. As she tells Schumann, she knows that this truth in life has escaped her, but is convinced that it will be revealed, if at all, in a moment of extreme affliction, against all that she as a person could possibly desire, and that this constitutes for her a vocation, a vocation which can only be realised at the moment of death. She is afraid, she admits, of failing not in her life, but in her death (*EL* 214).

The idea of vocation is present too in the passage in the autobiographical letter to Father Perrin, where she evokes the same subject. Again, she suggests that this 'moment of truth' is in fact the moment of literal, physical death:

I have always believed that the moment of death is the norm

and the aim of my life. I have always felt that, for those who live appropriately, it is the moment when, for an infinitesimal fraction of time, pure, naked, certain, eternal truth enters the soul. I can say that I have never desired any other good for myself. I have always believed that the life which leads to this good is not defined simply by common morality, but that for every individual it consists in a succession of acts and events which is strictly personal, and so obligatory in nature that anyone who does not follow that succession misses the target. Such for me was the notion of vocation.[6]

It is apparent from these passages that there is an intimate relationship in Simone Weil's thinking between the concepts of affliction, death and the revelation of reality. She was at the same time acutely aware, as she makes clear, that this was a personal vocation. Admitting as much to Schumann, she puts it down to 'a physical defect in my nature', comparing herself unfavourably and apologetically to those who have normal aspirations and appetite for life. She thus illustrates once again the impossibility of treating her thought as pure 'philosophy', aside from lived experience. In her eyes, goodness was one and unique, but the paths leading to it were many and various. There is never any suggestion, quite the contrary in fact, that anyone else should follow the same vocation. Although affliction can reveal reality, not only can one not seek it out for oneself, but one should do all in one's power to prevent others being thrown into it: if people who are not ready for it or do not have the necessary vocation come into contact with affliction, they risk being destroyed before they have the chance to consent to it, just as the destructive effect of modern factory conditions precluded any spiritual value to the work done there.

There is a notion related to that of affliction and physical death which should be evoked here, and that is what Simone Weil called 'decreation' ('décréation'). It is part of man's quest for goodness, his response to God's act of creation. As we have seen, by creation, God permitted something other than Himself to exist, and created individuals, by their very individuality, are in opposition to the will of God (*C*2 241). The individual must therefore renounce his capacity to say 'I', so that God and creation can again be one. For Simone Weil this is destructive only in so far as it concerns the illusory 'I': in the order of truth,

'I lie when I say "I"' ('Dire "je" c'est mentir'). By consenting to the destruction of the 'I', I only accept what has been true all the time, namely, that in terms of true being I do not exist anyway. 'God created me as non-being appearing to exist, so that, by renouncing through love this apparent existence, I may be annihilated in the fullness of being.'[7] Decreation thus reveals the truth of our existence.

It is obvious that, while this process may involve physical death, it does not necessarily do so. Simone Weil speaks of it elsewhere as a 'moral death', which she defines as consenting to be subject to anything that fate can impose (*CS* 175). There is virtually nothing in me that cannot be destroyed by accidental circumstance: the only permanent feature is my faculty of consent to destruction. Reality is therefore what is left when everything else has been stripped away, and that naturally includes everything that is personal to me. Simone Weil's reasoning seems to be that because I as an individual am not an essential and permanent part of the order of things, I therefore do not count, except by giving my free consent to the world-order. This, be it said in passing, explains her predilection in the natural world for phenomena expressing the laws of nature, for the waves on the sea or the folds in the mountains. Although capable of being deeply moved by natural phenomena such as these, she was not interested, as far as one can tell, in the individual features of nature. In the vast collection of jottings with which she filled her notebooks, almost the only references to named plants, trees, or animals are those which have some significance in myth or folktale, or which are symbolic in some way. The world-order is what matters, and to that she gave her total adherence. The 'no' to the individual self seems to be in many ways the inevitable price to be paid for an unreserved 'yes' to the whole world of the rest of creation.

The question of Simone Weil's own death should perhaps be raised again at this point. It has sometimes been suggested that she died as an inevitable result of the decreative process to which she subjected herself. Paradoxically, there may be truth in this in so far as the conditions she found in London were totally other than what she would have wanted for herself — at least for the superior part of her soul, as she would have said — since she was deprived of the possibility of following what she saw as her vocation. But therein lies the inadequacy of such an explanation.

She was perfectly aware that a part of her, the animal part which she had spent her life taming and bringing under control, still relished the comparative comfort and safety of the job she was given to do. Decreation was a process by which that part was to be totally eliminated, put to death, where the individual desiring will is gradually subsumed into the eternal order of the universe. That process could not take place, she felt, unless she had her part, a very large part, in affliction, even though the natural part of her could not possibly will this participation. Her vocation meant that she was utterly convinced that such participation was an order from God — she says somewhere that obedience to that kind of order is everything, even if one is mistaken in its content. What she lacked, therefore, in London, was the possibility for true decreation, for respecting that higher part of herself which desired absolute goodness and, as a corollary, true knowledge. Deprived of participation in the affliction of the times, she could only impose increasing hardship on herself in what she felt to be a futile but necessary gesture of solidarity. She did not aim to die: but death became a kind of inevitable alternative to decreation — which would probably, however, sooner or later, have brought death in its wake.

The concept of decreation can also help in the interpretation of the terrible 'example of prayer' which she gives in the New York notebooks (*CS* 204–5), and which understandably so shocks commentators. In it she asks that all her mental and physical faculties be destroyed, leaving her in a state of idiocy, incapable of rational thought or affective response to any creature whatever. At the same time, she asks that her body and all her faculties operate in perfect conformity to God's will, that her intelligence be a perfect vehicle for absolute truth, and that she be sensitive in the highest degree possible to every shade of pain and joy. Furthermore she demands that her transformed faculties should then be torn from her, changed by God into the very substance of Christ, and given as nourishment to the afflicted, leaving her in a state of total incapacity. All this she asks *as if* she truly desired it, knowing however that it is impossible to desire such destruction for the self. What she is doing here is merely spelling out in uncompromising detail what she suggests time and again elsewhere: that her vocation is to be no more than a passage, a tool for Christ to come to the aid of the afflicted. But how difficult it was for her even to confide such thoughts to her personal notebooks is shown in the note immediately following the 'example of prayer': she claims in some desperation that such spiritual matters are totally beyond her competence, reserved for people who possess for a start what she calls 'elementary moral virtues'. She can only talk at random about them — and is not even capable of saying sincerely that she is talking at random.

Simone Weil indicates certain techniques for bringing about the process of decreation which results in the destruction of the self. One of these relates to the particular way in which she views human energy. Energy for Simone Weil is divided into two sorts, 'vegetative energy', which sustains biological life, and 'supplementary energy', which provides the motive force for will and desire, and allows us to 'escape' from difficult or painful situations (*CS* 178). When a situation becomes intolerable, however, supplementary energy is exhausted, and the energy that sustains life itself is exposed and begins to be used up. It is then, according to Simone Weil, that the soul, threatened in its very existence, cries 'Enough!', but it is also precisely at that moment that it must consent to the intolerable situation continuing indefinitely. A quarter of an hour spent in this state is more revealing of reality than years spent trying to improve oneself, she claims.

The discipline of accepting the unacceptable is part of what could be termed in Simone Weil's philosophy acceptance of the void. It is characteristic of her that she takes a term from the mechanical sciences, that of the vacuum, and applies it to the workings of human psychology. What is interesting about her use of it, however, is that the vacuum is something unnatural. For the Ancient Greeks, too, a vacuum was 'impossible', since it would cause suffering to the cosmos, just as for Simone Weil psychological void causes man to suffer. Extreme suffering always creates a feeling of impossibility, according to her, and this impossibility is the feeling of the void itself (*C2* 22). Void is what results 'when nothing exterior corresponds to an interior tension' (*C2* 111), when a desire is perpetually unsatisfied and one is therefore exposed to 'the total pressure of the surrounding universe' (*C2* 119).

The experience of the void can be either voluntary or involuntary. In the former case, it occurs when an individual recognises that no object here on earth can satisfy his desire for good, and he deliberately refuses a natural inclination towards satisfaction. In the latter, one experiences void in particular when exposed to affliction, or to any intolerable situation, when one's whole natural being refuses what is happening. The eternal round of working to exist, and existing in order to work, that was her experience of factory work, is another example of void in practice: it is intolerable, she says, to spend so much energy to find oneself back at the same point afterwards (*C*2 44). We need compensation, a reward, for effort expended (*C*2 99), so much so that suffering in the mind can be defined as producing 'efforts in a void' (*C*2 117).

Clearly, since the experience of the void is so against nature, the natural tendency of anyone in such a situation is to try to get out of it as quickly as possible. The means of doing this are always, for Simone Weil, related to the imagination. In her view, the imagination is always a negative faculty, because it is a way of avoiding reality. When a person finds himself in a situation which is unacceptable, the immediate reaction of the imagination is to escape into the past or the future and create a different scenario. If this is not possible, there is generated a feeling of impossibility, of disequilibrium, in which this remodelling of past, future and otherwise remote phenomena does not take place (*C*2 79).

The imagination is thus at the root of all attempts to flee reality, and since, for Simone Weil, the acceptance of reality is virtue itself, its non-acceptance is the equivalent of sin. Hence: 'Void is what makes man capable of sin. All sins are attempts to conquer void' (*C*2 18). The mechanism of this psychological void is as clear and inevitable as that of the physical vacuum: a tension is created which needs to be broken, and the evil which an individual perpetrates in this situation is the direct result of that tension. The desire for vengeance, for example, is a desire for equilibrium, an almost physical need to hit back in order to break the void within oneself created by the harm that someone has done. Even if this desire is not satisfied, the imagination, by creating an equivalent escape, restores the lost equilibrium. If this is evil, then its contrary, virtue, is an acceptance of disequilibrium. For example, not exercising all the power at one's disposal is an acceptance of void (*C*2 33). Idolatry, in the rather special sense Simone Weil gives to it, is a direct result of the phenomenon of void, whether in its social form — she gives the seventeenth-century idolising of the great as an example — or its modern equivalent, the idolising of money. Her fine sense of human motivation comes to the fore when she considers the different attitudes which can be adopted towards leader-figures, in this case, Christ and Napoleon (*C*2 16). It was easy, she says, to be faithful to Napoleon, because he was a figure of power and prestige. On the other hand, faithfulness to Christ at the moment of his death was almost impossible, it was 'faithfulness in a void' ('fidélité à vide'), because he was crucified as a common criminal, afflicted, stripped of power and divinity. Later, she says, it was easy for Christian martyrs to go to their death, because they had the prestige of the Church behind them. One dies for what is strong, not for what is weak. They also had the consolation of an assured future life ahead of them, and consolations, for Simone Weil, are always attempts to overcome void. She gives a striking example from her experience in the Spanish Civil War, when the Militia would sometimes invent victories that had never happened, in order to protect themselves from the fear of death, and from the knowledge that their cause was not victorious.

The thought of death, especially certain death, is a powerful creator of void, and therefore properly unthinkable. We cannot truly conceive of our own death, save perhaps for a few moments of horror, because with death all motives are suppressed, all projection into the future rendered impossible. A similarly brutal severance of the future can occur for other reasons, death of a loved one, betrayal, the sudden loss of something on which the thought of the future was strongly dependent. Always it is a deprivation of the power to project, a forced suppression of the imagination.

The relationship between the acceptance of the void — the refusal to project, to take possession of past and future, and to give in to the promptings of the imagination — and the concept of decreation, is an obvious one. In the process of decreation the individual self is renounced, not in a spirit of self-discipline for its own sake, but in the interests of a greater reality, just as an acceptance of void is consent to the way things really are. There is the same ambiguous relationship with death: sometimes it seems that Simone Weil is talking about real, physical death — and always in any case implies a necessary acceptance of it — sometimes it is more accurately death of the individual expansive self. 'To resolve to die, and to accept the void, are the same thing: that alone, in certain situations, prevents lies from being a vital necessity.'[8] But the ambiguity of the relationship between real physical death and that brought about by decreation is illustrated when Simone Weil says: 'Death itself, undergone for a bad cause, is not really death for the carnal part of the soul. Seeing God face to face is death for the carnal part of the soul./That is why we flee internal void, because God could slip into it.[9]

Simone Weil does not therefore envisage the void as simple privation. It is that, certainly, but it is also a condition for the descent of grace. Because we fear the presence of absolute good, we exercise ourselves through our imagination in an attempt to block up the holes through which grace could pass (*C*1 276), producing compensations of all kinds to prevent a void from being created. We need a reward for what we have done, a restoration of equilibrium following effort expended. If we do violence to that psychological necessity, we leave a void, and a supernatural reward descends. If, however, we have already received our reward, there is no room for it to descend (*C*1 267). If this seems mechanical, it should be pointed out that Simone Weil is acutely aware of the dangers of exposing people to the experience of the void, and of the ambivalence of such an experience. Affliction can either be the experience of reality itself — or the definitive destruction of all that is best in a human being. In the same way, she insists that void should be eliminated as far as possible from social life: it is too spiritually dangerous an experience for the great mass of humanity, and there will always be enough for those that need it.

If, however, the experience of the void can be positive in the manner in which it can open the way to spiritual reward, it is only in so far as we do not attempt to define the content of this reward. 'It is by desiring truth in the void, without trying to guess in advance its content, that we receive light', she says.[10] One cannot overestimate the importance of the concept of desire in Simone Weil's philosophy: desire, for her, creates reality, at least in the domain of absolute goodness. Her earliest recorded spiritual insight, dating, as she says, from the time when she thought she was an atheist, was the conviction that if one desires absolute truth intensely enough one will be rewarded: if one desires bread one does not receive stones.

An equally important concept, and one which depends on desire for its efficacy, is that of attention, familiar to any reader of Simone Weil. It is one of her profoundest insights, and not limited to the narrowly religious sphere. In so far as the revelation of truth depends on it, she makes the formation of attention the main aim of school studies. It is also the only basis for true relationships between people, whether between friends or between an observer and an anonymous passer-by in some kind of need or distress, in that it reveals the true reality of the other. Attention is the opening to truth which comes from the outside, opposed to all acts of will, and to all muscular effort: 'Attention consists in suspending thought, leaving it available, empty and ready to be entered by its object ... thought must be empty, waiting, seeking nothing, but ready to receive in its naked truth the object that is about to penetrate it'.[11]

It is an opening up of the soul, but to an unspecified object: even in the case where the object is a person whom I may think I know well, Simone Weil claims, paying attention means that I really look and really listen, without imposing my preconceived ideas on that person. In this way, the mind becomes a simple recipient for the truth that enters into it, and not a creator of truth. I cannot create truth, I can only desire it and then consent to its presence in me. But although this approach is apparently negative, it is in fact the only way to make contact with reality. Simone Weil quotes with approval a series of techniques from Taoist philosophy where, for example, a hunter trains himself never to miss his prey, however small, provided he has attained a particular degree of attention. Thus 'a certain quality of attention is linked to effective movement, with neither effort nor desire'.[12] In another sense, however, 'attention is linked to desire. Not to will, but to desire' (*PG* 136) — provided one remembers that it is a question of desire without an object. The notion she is attempting to define here has affinities with the *advertencia amorosa* ('loving attention') of St John of the Cross, a loving opening to God, not attached either to any earthly object or to any particular goal. As for St John of the Cross, for Simone Weil also it was not a question of suppressing desire, but rather of emptying it of its normal object. We need the energy provided by desire, she says, but its use must be transformed. We must go to the root of desire in order to tear energy away from its object. Desire is real, it is only its objects that are false. This tearing away process is a condition of truth (*C*2 86–7). Inevitably it hurts: the attachment of desire to its object is very powerful, as in the case of the miser and his treasure, or a woman and her lover (*C*3 97). We direct our energy into a desired object, and the loss of the object causes the energy previously focused to be released into the void — what she calls the unreal void, nothingness (*C*3 99). Detachment, conversely, is the release of the totality of that energy towards God, as absolute goodness rather than specific object. From our particular perspective, this absolute can only be conceived as void. Our task is simply to turn our attention in the right direction, necessitating a 'long apprenticeship' during which we experience the 'dark night of the soul', to borrow another expression from St John of the Cross. At the end of this 'night', however, there is a transformation: the void which from a natural point of view was experienced as privation, as emptiness, is now seen to be fullness itself, supreme plenitude, the source and principle of all reality (*C*3 120). As so often in Simone Weil's thought, a change of perspective brings about a radical change in perception.

What Simone Weil is talking about here is clearly the object of mystical experience itself, and it is characteristic of her that, as with her own mystical experiences, she does not evoke it often. When referring to the void, it is much more often in terms of its negative: the experience of emptiness resulting from the deliberate or enforced suppression of goals or objects of desire. This is partly through a natural diffidence when talking about ultimate spiritual experience, partly also no doubt through a reluctance to evoke anything which might be construed as a consolation to the human predicament. 'The void is the supreme plenitude', she claims, 'but man does not have the right to know it' (*CS* 113). Christ himself was deprived of this knowledge at one moment. In Simone Weil's belief, it is essential to start off from the position of privation, where the imagination has been suppressed and no compensations are available. In its distress, the soul can only cry out 'Why? Why this suffering?' Only when the soul has understood that the created universe has no answer to that question, that the finality it seeks does not exist on earth, can the true nature of the void it is experiencing be revealed. Simone Weil explains the process:

> The soul which, because it is torn apart by affliction, continues to cry out for this finality, touches the void. If it does not give up loving, it will hear one day not the answer to the question it is crying out, for there is none, but silence itself as something infinitely more full of meaning than any answer, as the very word of God.[13]

Paradox indeed, but it is only through paradox that Simone Weil can express ultimately a reality which is only tentatively bound to the language of normal rational discourse, where what has no definition is alone real, and where the void is perfect fullness.

Several important features stand out, I think, from this analysis. The first is Simone Weil's constant desire to confront in all their stark reality the least acceptable aspects of the human condition. She neither involves herself in the contradiction of making them the responsibility of a beneficent creator-God, nor, in spite of her social concerns, tries to reform them out of existence or politicise them. Nor does she simply bemoan them: rather, she uses them in a highly personal construction of a moral order.

At the same time, she makes mystical experience a coherent part of life in its totality, not an aberrant form of knowledge accessible only to those who shut themselves off from life as lived by ordinary people. Affliction which, as she saw in her everyday experience, is the lot of too great a proportion of humanity, could be a way to knowledge of supernatural goodness, but only when totally without consolation.

It is this last point which raises doubts as to the possibility of extending her use of affliction beyond her own very particular vocation. Her desire to partake of the sufferings of humanity in general is, after all, only an extension, an unusually generous one but not unknown in others, of the natural human tendency to want to share in the affliction of loved ones. She felt the affliction of anonymous individuals thousands of miles away in the same way that ordinary, decent human beings feel that of relatives and friends: they, too, feel somehow better when they can be there to share and console. But Simone Weil's extraordinary lucidity, her total commitment to truth as she saw it, however radically unacceptable in normal terms, and her consequent refusal of consolation in any form whatever, betoken a very particular vocation which is shared by few. She paid the price for this vocation, while devoting a good deal of her thought to ways in which others without her vocation could have access to that spirituality which was the birthright of every human being.

Notes

1. *Cl* 11: 'Je crois à la valeur de la souffrance dans la mesure où l'on fait tout (ce qui est honnête) pour l'éviter' (Simone Weil's parentheses).
2. *Cl* 27: '*N'oublie jamais que tu as le monde tout entier, la vie tout entière devant toi . . . Que, pour toi, la vie peut et doit être plus réelle, plus pleine et plus joyeuse qu'elle n'a été peut-être pour aucun être humain . . . Ne la mutile d'avance par aucun renoncement. Ne te laisse mettre en prison par aucune affection*' (Simone Weil's italics).
3. *EL* 214: 'Car ma nature est lâche. Tout ce qui est pénible et dangereux me fait peur'.
4. *AD* 82: 'Le malheur est un déracinement de la vie, un équivalent plus ou moins atténué de la mort, rendu irrésistiblement présent à l'âme par l'atteinte ou l'appréhension immédiate de la douleur physique'.
5. *AD* 85: '[Le malheur [. . .] imprime jusqu'au fond de l'âme [. . .]] ce mépris, ce dégoût et même cette répulsion de soi-même, cette sensation de culpabilité et de souillure, que le crime devrait logiquement produire et ne produit pas'.
6. *AD* 33: 'J'ai toujours cru que l'instant de la mort est la norme et le but de la vie. Je pensais que pour ceux qui vivent comme il convient, c'est l'instant où pour une fraction infinitésimale du temps la vérité pure, nue, certaine, éternelle entre dans l'âme. Je peux dire que jamais je n'ai désiré pour moi un autre bien. Je pensais que la vie qui mène à ce bien n'est pas définie seulement par la morale commune, mais que pour chacun elle consiste en une succession d'actes et d'événements qui lui est rigoureusement personnelle, et tellement obligatoire que celui qui passe à côté manque le but. Telle était pour moi la notion de vocation'.
7. *CS* 42: 'Dieu m'a créée comme du non-être qui a l'air d'exister, afin qu'en renonçant par amour à cette existence apparente, la plénitude de l'être m'anéantisse'.
8. *Cl* 276: '*ETRE RÉSOLU A MOURIR, ACCEPTER LE VIDE, MEME CHOSE; CELA SEUL PERMET QUE, DANS CERTAINES SITUATIONS, LE MENSONGE NE SOIT PAS UNE NÉCESSITÉ VITALE*' (Simone Weil's capitals).

9. *C3* 270: 'La mort même, subie pour une cause mauvaise, n'est pas vraiment la mort pour la partie charnelle de l'âme. Ce qui est mort pour la partie charnelle de l'âme, c'est de voir Dieu face à face./C'est pourquoi nous fuyons le vide intérieur, parce que Dieu pourrait s'y glisser'.
10. *EL* 139: 'C'est en désirant la vérité à vide et sans tenter d'en deviner d'avance le contenu qu'on reçoit la lumière'.
11. *AD* 76–7: 'L'attention consiste à suspendre sa pensée, à la laisser disponible et pénétrable à l'objet ... la pensée doit être vide, en attente, ne rien chercher, mais être prête à recevoir dans sa vérité nue l'objet qui va y pénétrer'.
12. *C2* 43: 'Une certaine qualité d'attention est liée aux mouvements efficaces, sans effort ni désir'.
13. *IP* 168: 'L'âme qui, parce qu'elle est déchirée par le malheur, crie continuellement après cette finalité, touche ce vide. Si elle ne renonce pas à aimer, il lui arrive un jour d'entendre non pas une réponse à la question qu'elle crie, car il n'y en a pas, mais le silence même comme quelque chose d'infiniment plus plein de signification qu'aucune réponse, comme la parole même de Dieu'.

6 Mediators and Mediation

Simone Weil's thought in the end seems to revolve around two poles, at one and the same time distinct and yet totally dependent one on the other. The one, to which we have already given a good deal of attention, is the gulf which she posits between the order of necessity to which the whole of creation is subject, and the order of goodness to which all men by nature aspire, and her deep mistrust of anything which appears to confuse the two. The other is the means by which absolute goodness can in fact illuminate the domain of necessity, through the mediation of perfectly pure phenomena, or phenomena which become pure because of a change in human perspective. Mediation plays, in fact, a crucial role in Simone Weil's thinking, allowing both human aspiration to ascend to its true object, and absolute goodness to descend in the form of grace, and showing once again how essential it was for her that even spiritual reality should pass the test of matter. Mediation is thus not some abstract concept for the delectation of philosophers, but part, and a vital part, of Simone Weil's programme for the reform of society: mediation was to be sought in every area of life, on the factory floor, in relationships between individuals, in the products of man's artistic life, as in his grasp of the physical universe around him.

The notions of the void, and in particular of decreation, which we have been considering in the foregoing pages, are essential also to an understanding of mediation. It is only when I have withdrawn from my illusory place in the centre of the universe, when I have in other words decreated my desiring and projecting self, that I am capable of viewing phenomena as mediators, just as it is only when I maintain the void and refuse to phenomena the status of legitimate objects of desire that room is left for grace to descend. Mediation depends therefore on perspective; it is not a permanent feature either of my mind or of the world around me, but a function of the relationship I establish with the world.

This can be seen clearly in the way in which, in certain circumstances, necessity itself can mediate between human beings and absolute goodness. Normally, as we have seen, necessity is experienced by man, in Simone Weil's view of things, either as hostile, in conflict with an individual's needs or desire — it represents danger, as in the sea which can wreck ships or drown people, or lightning which can kill through unpredictability — or, at the very least, as something to be reckoned with, an element to be conquered by man, for example in the exhausting efforts he has to make in manual work. In this case, a kind of equilibrium can be established between man and necessity, so that while its harshness is still apparent, necessity is no longer experienced simply as crushing brutality. Nevertheless, as Simone Weil says: 'Necessity is an enemy for man as long as he thinks in the first person'.[1] A first stage away from regarding it thus is when we realise that what we experience as force is also what she calls 'the very object of mathematics' (*IP* 146), in other words, a network of relationships, pure and theoretical. When we see it in this way, it is no longer an enemy — but it remains something exterior to us, imposing conditions on us. It is precisely because it is exterior, does not conform to our will, remains eternally the same whatever we do or think, that it can become an intermediary, in Simone Weil's view. The only faculty we have that is not subject to necessity is our consent, and by consenting to it as pure obedience to the will of God, our perspective changes, and we are raised to a higher plane. Simone Weil explains:

> While we think in the first person, we see necessity from below, from inside; it shuts us in on every side like the surface of the earth and the vault of the sky. As soon as we abandon thinking in the first person by consenting to necessity, we see it from the outside, beneath us, for we have passed to the side where God is. The side which it showed to us beforehand, and which it still shows to almost the whole of our being, to our natural part, is brutal dominance. The side which it shows after this operation to that fragment of our thought which has passed to the other side is pure obedience.[2]

Note that necessity has not itself changed in any way: it is simply our relationship with it that has. It is thus not true to say that the supernatural descends into matter, but rather that matter, nature itself, is changed through the presence of the supernatural (*IP* 163). Necessity, being the meeting-point between matter whose order it conveys and the supernatural, becomes a mediator in several different ways: it is an intermediary between our nature and our faculty of free consent, and it also mediates between those things whose order it reflects and God, and between those things themselves, in so far as each thing being in its appointed place within a given order allows each other thing to exist in the same way.

Simone Weil is aware, however, of the rarified nature of these speculations, and of the fact that mathematical necessity revealing the order of the world, because it is recognised by mind alone, is likely to have a limited appeal to people other than mathematicians — although she had great faith in the capacity of very ordinary intellects to grasp mathematical truth. For its appeal to be universal, mathematical necessity must touch the body and the senses also; this it does, she says, through beauty. 'What allows us to contemplate necessity and love it is the beauty of the world.'[3] The consent which we give to necessity is possible only through a certain complicity with the natural and physical part of ourselves, and the fullness of that complicity is the fullness of joy. We have already noted Simone Weil's conception of beauty, and it is important to underline here again that it is not strictly speaking an aesthetic category, or at least that her approach to beauty, whether natural or artistic, is never mere aestheticism. Because, as a true Platonist, she considered beauty to be the physical manifestation of goodness, the reflection of goodness in matter, it was a revelation of order and reality as much as anything else. She is insistent that beauty is not an attribute of matter, but rather a relationship between the world of matter and our sensibility; it is, in other words, a matter of perception. She is thoroughly Stoic here: by suppressing my individual desire to change the world, she claims, by retreating on a personal level to allow the created world simply to be, I love it as order: as she says, the beauty of the world is the order of the world when it is loved. Through beauty, matter is enabled to partake of goodness, and acts thus as mediator between the two orders. Although this may seem a somewhat abstract way of looking at the beautiful, the idea of beauty revealing order in fact accounts for both natural beauty in a very obvious way, and various forms of beauty in art, whether of a plastic, literary or musical kind. Because it is the manifestation of reality itself, its characteristics are both intellectual and physical.

Convinced that myth and folklore are the expression first and foremost of spiritual truth, Simone Weil interprets the Greek myth of Persephone as an account of the way in which, through beauty, God 'traps' the unsuspecting soul and opens it to grace. Persephone, daughter of the earth-mother Demeter, was captured by Hades, god of the Underworld, as a consequence of picking a narcissus while playing alone one day. The mourning of the mother for her daughter prevented the crops from growing, and finally Hades relented and sent Persephone back to earth, but not before she had eaten the fatal pomegranate seed, which made her his wife for ever. In Simone Weil's interpretation, the narcissus represents beauty, the 'trap' used by God to attract the soul. The pomegranate seed represents the consent which the soul gives to God, almost in spite of itself, the 'infinitely small' which nevertheless decides its destiny eternally. These two moments are crucial to Simone Weil's view of the salvation process, the one when the soul is 'trapped' in all innocence, reacting quite spontaneously on all levels of its being, without realising what it is doing, the other when consent is given, although again it is consent to something of which the soul remains ignorant, since if Persephone had known the consequences of her action, she would never have eaten the seed. The myth is thus an excellent illustration of the way in which Simone Weil gives vital relevance to such ancient folk-tales, as well as giving a clear account of her approach to the mystical way. What is remarkable, and should be underlined, is the way in which it joins her thinking on every level: in every aspect of life we are subject in large measure to forces outside ourselves and over which we have no control, forces which frequently seem hostile to our individual desires, and to which our reaction is almost entirely passive. We have, however, one active role to play, and that is to consent to these forces — frequently consent for Simone Weil is seen as a continuing process, rather than a single moment of acceptance. But consent, that combination of intelligence and love which for Simone Weil represents the highest level in the structure of a human being, is impossible without an appeal to that part of one that responds to physical beauty.

This series of imperatives is particularly noticeable in the world of work, to which Simone Weil devoted so much of her time and attention. There, as we have seen, the worker is subject the whole time to necessity, he is obliged at every moment to take account of the various forces he is manipulating, his own strength and capabilities, the particular requirements of the machine and the material he is transforming, the product he is aiming at. The lack of finality in his life, the obligation to perform the same routine day in, day out, merely to exist, creates a void which is perhaps as painful as hunger itself. Only one thing can make this monotony bearable, claims Simone Weil, and that is beauty, reflecting the light of eternity (*CO* 265). The contemplation of beauty is the only case in which a person can bear to reflect on what is, rather than what might be. 'Working people need poetry as they need bread', she declares. However, this is not the poetry of words which, by itself, can be of no use to them; their need is rather that the everyday substance of their lives should itself be poetry. Not surprisingly, we find her claiming that such poetry can have only one source, which is God: true poetry in the situation in which working people find themselves can only be religion. It is, in fact, their privilege, she maintains: in other situations particular aims are proposed to a specific activity, which form as it were a screen between the individual and God. For manual workers there is no such screen: they have only to look up. But that, she says, is the difficulty. Working people lack intermediaries, and it is no good therefore simply telling them to think about God. Even in church, people need objects to focus their attention: the architecture of the church, the liturgy and ritual gestures, the objects with which they are surrounded, all these act as mediators towards spiritual reality. There is nothing of this in the factory, where everything conspires to chain thought to earth. It is obviously neither possible nor desirable to introduce specifically religious symbols into the factory, but nor is it necessary: the role of mediator can be played by the very objects of work, the materials, the instruments and the gestures of work, by finding in them 'a reflecting property'. It is not a question of inventing fictions, but of 'reading the symbols which are written into matter from all eternity'(*CO* 276). We have already seen the way in which she wants to re-interpret Biblical parables to make them again relevant to the modern agricultural worker. For the industrial worker, Simone Weil feels that the symbols are ready there in the forces which he manipulates. Her interpretation of the lever is a good example of the way in which she interprets the physical as symbol of the spiritual. A lever, she says, is an illustration of the principle that movement downwards is a condition of ascent, and we have already noted the way she applies this concept to the spiritual domain, making it an image of the mechanical process by which the soul enters into contact with the supernatural. It becomes a symbol of decreated action itself in the following development:

> Stone in the way — Throw oneself on the stone, as if given a certain intensity of desire (effort is but desire) it ought no longer to exist. Or go away, as if one didn't exist oneself.
> Think together the existence of the stone as a limited object, and oneself as a limited being, and the relationship between the two; lever. If one simply pushes the lever, any effort becomes useless.
> We must be detached from desire to understand the equivalence, by transposition, between descent and upwards movement.[4]

The lever is thus an example of detachment, of renunciation of the world and of our desires with regard to it. For man in his natural state, 'desire leaps in time over intermediaries' (*C*2 34), whereas decreated man learns that 'to be able to conceive of intermediaries, one must maintain a *void*'.

Applying the concept to a more specifically Christian context, the lever is also the mechanical principle at the heart of the spiritual reality which is the Cross of Christ. The Cross was a balance where the body of Christ was a counter-weight to that of the universe (*IP* 178): Christ belongs to Heaven, and the distance between Heaven and the point of intersection of the branches of the Cross is to the distance from that point to earth as the weight of the world is to the weight of the body of Christ. One cannot help feeling again here that Simone Weil is at her best when discerning psychological law in the mechanical universe — in other words, simply affirming that all phenomena, people's minds as much as anything else, are subject to the same physical laws — and less happy when restricting these to a specifically Christian context, where the universal relevance of her observations seems to be lost. Even when she picks up mystical notions of movement which date back to medieval times and beyond, there is a universality in her viewpoint which at least commands attention, as for example in her comments on the difference between circular and oscillating movement. Oscillating movement, she contends, is an image of the human condition: we are composed, through our desires, of 'movements towards the exterior', but since we are limited creatures, these desires eventually reach a limit and are forced back upon us. In God, on the other hand, there is only eternal unchanging movement which comes full circle and has no object other than itself. Our oscillation is in fact a degraded image of this self-orientation which is exclusively divine (*CO* 268).

Far from being quaint evocations of an earlier age, such notions are for Simone Weil a crucial means of restoring the unity between manual and intellectual work. 'The point of unity between intellectual and manual work is contemplation, which is not work', she says (*CO* 270), and any reform of working conditions must aim at that 'contemplation'. The attention necessary for manual work can never be the same as that required by a theoretical problem, but if everyone exercises the kind of attention necessary for the work in hand, there will be fostered 'another kind of attention above all social obligation, which constitutes a direct link with God'.[5]

When Simone Weil turns from the world of manual work to that of mathematics, she does not hesitate to use there too an interpretative symbolism which originates from pre-Christian times, and can appear surprising in a modern scientific context. Following Plato, she considers mathematical knowledge to be at an intermediate level between the knowledge obtainable by the senses and that of 'dialectic', or 'pure thought'. It is in any case capable of revealing spiritual truth, and the modern world in her view is the poorer for having wanted to separate science and spirituality. Mathematics is not only a science mediating between two other forms of knowledge but, as it developed under Pythagoras and his disciples, it was in itself a search for mediation. It is her belief that the appearance of geometry in Greece was in fact a prophecy of Christ. Her assertion is based on a number of very complex demonstrations which we need not go into here, but certain points can be made in order to bring out the essentials of her argument. For a start, she holds that for the Pythagoreans number refers not to the means by which we count in a series, but to relationship, proportion. This is not impossible, given that

141

many of their theories depend on discoveries made in music, concerning the relationship of the strings of the lyre. Number is thus what establishes a relationship between a given number and unity, in other words, a mediating term. Secondly, she holds that one of the fundamental discoveries of the Pythagoreans was that of the 'irrational numbers', those numbers that have no natural relationship with unity, that is to say numbers that are not squares. They solved this through geometry, through the well-known 'Pythagorean theorem', where a right-angled triangle is inscribed within a circle, thus creating a proportional mean. For Simone Weil, this is the image of a supernatural mediation between God and man, an 'irrational number' who has no natural link with God. For a link to be created, a mediating term has to come from outside, as it does for the irrational numbers, 'images of our wretchedness' (*CO* 268). Thirdly, Simone Weil points to a specific connection between mathematical and religious thinking when she identifies the Greek word for number, *arithmos*, with the word which she says was used synonymously by the Greeks for the same phenomenon, *logos*. In John's Gospel in particular, *logos*, translated 'word', is the name given to Christ himself.

Simone Weil is thus able to claim that Greek mathematics was a search for religious mediation, and that Christ was the result, both logically and historically, of their search. I will return to the figure of Christ, who is obviously of major importance to Simone Weil, but first it should be noted that she finds in myth and ancient tradition generally many of the same kind of 'prophecies' that she finds in Pythagorean geometry. There is a whole group of Middle Eastern vegetation gods, for instance, whose ritual death and resurrection, following the cycle of the seasons, Simone Weil associates with the death and resurrection of Christ. One of the best-known of these is Dionysos, whose cult was at the centre of the Greek Mystery religions. Others, among the many gods whom she evokes, are Zagreus, the child-god of Crete, and Osiris, the Egyptian god, who also died and was resurrected. They have in common their suffering, although Simone Weil does not seem to take account of the fact that there is no suggestion in Greek tradition that this was redemptive suffering. When she makes the figure of Prometheus a figure of Christ, she indeed underlines the idea that he suffered on behalf of humanity, for having loved mankind too much. His name, according to her, means 'for knowledge', which she associates with the Sophoclean 'knowledge through suffering'. The fire which he brought to earth for men, having stolen it from the gods, was the Holy Spirit itself. Simone Weil in fact sees in Prometheus all the mediating characteristics of Christ, with only the historical incarnation lacking. It is nevertheless the notion of incarnation which makes all these god-figures important to her: in one way or another they shared man's destiny, the myth depends on their capacity to suffer, whether or not an historical incarnation took place. A fundamental characteristic of mediators is that they are 'made flesh': even in the case of something so totally impersonal as beauty, it is essential to see it as incarnated in matter.

Another type of incarnation, and one which links up with the mechanistic view of the operation of the human mind which I have evoked earlier, is that relating to what Simone Weil calls 'the perfectly just man', or 'the perfectly pure being', who through redemptive suffering breaks a chain of evil action. She analyses the mechanism of this action thus: 'The contact with purity produces a transformation in evil. The indissoluble mixture of suffering and sin can be dissolved only by it. By this contact, bit by bit suffering ceases to be mixed with sin; on the other hand sin is transformed into simple suffering'.[6] Simone Weil finds a number of these perfectly pure beings in the Old Testament — they are among the few figures there that she accepts as having truly spiritual significance — among them Abel, Enoch, Noah, Shem, Nimrod, Daniel and Job. This last was for her of particular importance as a mediating figure because of his experience of affliction. Job experienced physical pain, moral outrage and social reprobation in a society where affliction was considered to be a consequence of sin, of disobedience towards God. Job's cry of 'Why should I suffer thus?' and his constant assertion of his innocence are those of every afflicted person, and it is because he refused all consolation — even the consolation of believing that his condition was a punishment for his own wrong-doing — that at the end of his 'dark night of the soul', in Simone Weil's interpretation, he was accorded the vision of the 'beauty of the world' (*C*2 157). She treats in the same way a passage in Plato's *Republic*, where he evokes a figure of perfect justice, but stripped of all prestige and having the appearance of injustice. In Plato's words, he will be tortured and crucified, appearing unjust, and it is only thus that he will in fact be just. Simone Weil establishes a parallel with Christ, who not only suffered, but suffered as a common criminal, uniting in himself perfect justice and the appearance of extreme injustice (*C*2 303). In fact, she concludes, such a figure must be God incarnate, since no other being can suffer injustice in this way without being altered by the evil he is suffering (*C*3 323).

It is certainly with this in mind that Simone Weil created the central character in her play, *Venise sauvée*. She states her aim as 'to take up again, for the first time since Greece, the tradition of the tragedy where the hero is perfect'.[7] We have already considered this play in the context of the revelation of beauty (Chapter 3 above), but the other main theme is that of redemptive suffering. Jaffier by his action in revealing the plot against Venice breaks the cycle of evil that would have resulted in its destruction, but at the same time takes all that evil on himself, transforming it into pure suffering. He goes to his death in a state of pure affliction, knowing that he as an individual must perish. In Simone Weil's terminology, he accepts void by refusing to pass on evil, refusing the compensations offered by the imagination. Crucial to Jaffier's affliction is the fact that he did not want it, did not even envisage it: he knew he would be punished, possibly even with death, for his part in the plot, but such suffering is not affliction. Affliction came when his companions were not spared, as he had been promised they would be, and when their belief that he had cynically betrayed them led to his total social reprobation.

If Jaffier is an image of Christ, and all the other figures which we have been considering are prefigurations of the Christian Saviour, it is nevertheless Christ himself who remains central to Simone Weil's philosophy, as to her experience. It is after all Christ who, as she relates, came down and took her during her recitation of George Herbert's 'Love', and all her subsequent mystical experiences have Christ at their centre. There is no doubt that, in the beautiful mystical prose-poem which stands as the Prologue to *La Connaissance surnaturelle*, the figure whose company she shared in the bare attic until ordered to leave by her unidentified host is again Christ. Her speculations in the area of religious philosophy should not obscure the fact that her own mystical experience was at the heart of this speculation, any more than her love for the religions of antiquity and other non-Christian traditions should blind us to the fact that the tradition to which she felt she belonged without a shadow of doubt was the Christian one, and at its centre was the figure of Christ.

Christ is thus for Simone Weil the point of contact of all the mediation-themes that I have been evoking, 'mediation itself', as she puts it (*IP* 163). He is, most obviously, Saviour, related to the other Saviour-gods of antiquity, and Simone Weil's interpretation pays little heed to the historicity or otherwise of these various traditions. It is perhaps because the historicity of Christ himself was not of central concern to her that she is able to assimilate him so easily to similar figures. She did not deny the historical incarnation — her interpretation of the symbolism of the Cross, for example, implies the meeting in the crucifixion of time and eternity — but she never gives the impression that it is of great importance. The ambivalence of her position is manifest in the following note: 'The story of Christ is a symbol, a metaphor. But people used to believe that metaphors occurred as events in the world. God is the supreme poet'.[8]

As in the case of other mediator-gods, the efficacy of the incarnation lies not so much in the incarnation itself, as in the suffering it entails. Incarnation, the separation of God from God, necessarily implies suffering, and it is this suffering which is completed in the affliction of the Cross. There, evil was transformed into pure suffering, and by that transformation became redemptive. By assimilation to the Cross of Christ salvation is possible, through the knowledge of reality which the suffering of the Cross brings about. The whole of Simone Weil's meditation on the nature of affliction comes to rest at the foot of the Cross, and in many ways it is sufficient for her: she does not need the triumph of the resurrection. The death of Christ represents the ultimate victory of force over spirit, which is weak by definition. Success or earthly conquest are, as we have seen, incompatible with spirituality. Death is thus the proof of the absolute spirituality of Christ, whereas resurrection is in a sense his victory over his enemies, but won on their territory. According to Simone Weil, spirit can never beat force on its own ground, since if it did it would represent a superior force, and thus have no relationship with absolute goodness.

The way in which Simone Weil sees Christ on the Cross as

mediating between God and man is of course perfectly traditional. She is less so when she makes him mediator between God and matter. The idea of Christ on the Cross being reduced to inert matter evokes her theory of force, and of the way in which it can reduce a man to the status of a mere thing. A man is reduced to matter when, as in the case of Christ, the circumstances preceding death have been sufficiently brutal, when he is truly afflicted (*IP* 131). When that man is also God, mediation is created between God and matter, because while being reduced to matter, he also retained his nature as God. This supreme union of opposites — nothing is more different from God than matter is — is possible through the supreme suffering of the Cross. Implied here also is the whole concept of decreation where, as we have seen, man becomes as inert matter in order to touch reality.

The presence of God in matter, which Simone Weil sees in the reduction of Christ to matter on the Cross, as well as in his incarnation in human form, is manifest also in the sacraments of the Church, an instance which it is worth evoking here as it underlines the immense importance of the sacraments for her in personal terms. The agonised question of her baptism was always considered by her as membership of the Church with a view to partaking of the sacraments. All her detailed questioning of priests and other members of the Church on the orthodoxy of her religious position underlines how crucial it was for her that her apprehension of the mysteries of the Christian religion be compatible with the Church's. She meditated deeply on her approach to the sacraments from her period in Marseilles onwards, as numerous notes and the essay on the 'theory of the sacraments' (*PSO* 134–47) bear witness. In the sacraments, God is again present in matter: Christ by his sacrifice offers himself to man in the form of flesh and blood. Our attitude to this, Simone Weil says, should be one of love rather than belief; it is this love which allows the soul to establish a contact with God through a simple piece of matter, and by love Christ becomes mediator in the Eucharist. 'To love Christ in the Eucharist is to meet him in it' (*C*2 147).

Simone Weil moves away from matter to the necessary relationships which govern it when she compares Christ to various mathematical notions. He is the proportional mean sought by the Pythagoreans, that which provides mediation between the irrational numbers and unity. He indicated as much himself, according to Simone Weil, by formulae expressing his relationship at one and the same time to God and man, such as 'As my Father has sent me, so send I you' (John 20, 21), a formula which, says Simone Weil, is also to be found in Plato where he describes mediation between God and man in terms of proportion. In the Gospel use of the term *logos* to designate Christ, Simone Weil also sees a connection with Greek mathematics since, as we have already seen, she considers *logos* and *arithmos* to have been equivalent for the Greeks, and *arithmos* was to be interpreted as meaning 'proportion'.

If this seems somewhat abstrusely theological, Simone Weil comes right back to the everyday concerns of ordinary people when she meditates on the role of Christ in relationships between people. Simone Weil was generally pessimistic on the submission of human relationships to force: when one party in a relationship is the stronger, the natural tendency is to make the other submit. This is extended in the idea of 'natural justice' when, due to there being equal or near-equal force on both sides, the parties come to an accommodation of interest. When this equal necessity is not present, however, justice can only be supernatural — Simone Weil calls it 'supernatural friendship'. She had the highest standards of friendship, recognising its rarity, and valuing it the more for this reason. Friendship, she says, occurs when the two individuals concerned renounce their capacity to say 'I', give up their position in the centre of the universe, and thus recognise the full existence of the other (*IP* 137–8). It is necessary because, although viewed from the outside, all human beings are equal, viewed from the perspective of the individual there is no greater disparity than that between that individual, who to himself is everything, and any other, who occupies a very restricted space relatively speaking. This renunciation is nothing other than the love of God, whether the thought of God be present or not. Thus, the 'renunciation of the power to think in the first person is the abandoning of all goods to follow Christ'.[9] This kind of love, or friendship, is for Simone Weil justice — again she finds in ancient Greek thought an equivalence between the two — and wherever it is to be found, Christ is the mediating principle. 'All true friendship passes through Christ' (*IP* 140).

Likewise love of one's neighbour needs the presence of Christ.

Simone Weil describes true love of one's neighbour as a withdrawal of the self so that Christ and the other can enter into contact. 'We should not come to the aid of our neighbour for Christ, but through Christ', she says (*C*2 268). Acts accomplished thus are necessarily good; the act is performed not with the thought of God in one's mind, however, but because attention given to the person in need has removed all possibility of acting otherwise. Simone Weil reflects thus on those who in the Gospel came to the aid of the needy: 'They were in a state in which they could not prevent themselves from feeding the hungry, clothing the naked; they did not in any way do it for Christ, they could not help doing it because the compassion of Christ was in them'.[10] This passage through Christ, or true charity, is nothing other than attention to absolute, absent good which, as we saw earlier, is the sole foundation of respect for other people. By maintaining one's attention fixed on absolute goodness, one allows at the same time this faculty to be developed in the other.

Christ is thus the supreme mediator between God and man. Other creatures, other objects can also play this role if, in one way or another, they imitate Christ. But it must be emphasised that this mediating role is not performed 'once and for all', there is no final resolution of the goodness–necessity opposition, and the apparent progression towards unity is misleading, since for Simone Weil duality and mediation are different aspects of the same reality. This is true to a paradoxical extent, because to understand truly the gulf between goodness and necessity is already to create a kind of mediation between them: one adopts a perspective from which reality is visible, and goodness manifests itself.

From this new perspective, the confusion between means and ends becomes impossible, the world and its creatures become a way, and the sense of exile is completed by the certainty of the reality — although not necessarily of the existence — of absolute goodness. This has clear implications for man's moral life, since the ethical and the intellectual perceptions are one and the same thing.

Another conclusion can be drawn concerning the nature of mediators themselves. If the idea of mediation depends on a particular perception, it is clear that the objects of mediation have no objective existence themselves. They exist, of course, as objects of perception, but to fulfil the role of mediators they depend on an individual's consciousness of the gulf between goodness and necessity, consciousness which implies the need of mediators and, as a result, mediators themselves. Mediation thus depends on a particular way of looking at the world.

Since people are not in their natural state conscious of the distance between goodness and necessity, the mediating role of other creatures is normally obscured. Mediation, as we have seen, necessitates decreation, that retreat of the self, which is such a crucial part of Simone Weil's philosophy. The suffering thus occasioned has a positive role, however, not only that of restoring the lost unity between God and man, but, through the disappearance of the autonomous 'I', creation can take on its essentially mediating function, the 'wound' between God and God brought about by the creative act is healed, and God is restored to God.

Thus the perception of God in the world, in beauty, in objects and creatures possessing perfect purity, can only follow and not precede the experience of the total absence of God. Only someone who has understood his fundamental exile in the world, and who has undergone 'the dark night of the soul', has access to the true presence of God. That that presence, which follows from the understanding of absence, was a reality for Simone Weil, there is no doubt. Her expression of the mystical union with God through his mediation in the world attains its climax in the following joyful affirmation (she is talking about the identity between Pythagorean 'relationship' and divine mediation): 'When one knows that, one knows that one lives in divine mediation, not like a fish in the sea, but like a drop of water in the sea. In us, outside us, here below, in the kingdom of God, nowhere is there anything else. And mediation is exactly the same thing as Love'.[11]

Notes

1. *IP* 144: 'La nécessité est une ennemie pour l'homme tant qu'il pense à la première personne'.
2. *IP* 153: 'Tant que nous pensons à la première personne, nous voyons la nécessité d'en dessous, du dedans; elle nous enferme de toutes

parts comme la surface de la terre et la voûte du ciel. Dès que nous renonçons à penser à la première personne par le consentement à la nécessité, nous la voyons du dehors, au-dessous de nous, car nous sommes passés du côté de Dieu. La face qu'elle nous présentait auparavant et qu'elle présente encore à notre être presque entier, à la partie naturelle de nous-mêmes, est domination brutale. La face qu'elle présente après cette opération à ce fragment de notre pensée qui est passé de l'autre côté est pure obéissance'.

3. *IP* 157: 'Ce qui permet de contempler la nécessité et de l'aimer, c'est la beauté du monde'.
4. *C2* 33: 'Pierre sur le chemin — Se jeter sur la pierre, comme si à partir d'une certaine intensité de désir (l'effort n'est que désir) elle devait ne plus exister. Ou s'en aller, comme si, soi-même, on n'existait pas./Penser ensemble l'existence et de la pierre comme chose limitée, et de soi comme être limité, et le rapport des deux; levier. Si on s'appuie simplement sur le levier, tout effort peut même être inutile./Il faut s'être détaché de son désir pour concevoir l'équivalence, par transposition, entre abaisser et élever'.
5. *CO* 271: '[On favorisera ainsi] une autre attention située au-dessus de toute obligation sociale, et qui constitue un lien direct avec Dieu'.
6. *PSO* 16: 'Le contact avec la pureté produit une transformation dans le mal. Le mélange indissoluble de la souffrance et du péché ne peut être dissocié que par lui. Par ce contact, peu à peu la souffrance cesse d'être mélangée de péché; d'autre part le péché se transforme en simple souffrance'.
7. *P* 52: 'Reprendre, pour la première fois depuis la Grèce, la tradition de la tragédie dont le héros est parfait'.
8. *CS* 149–50: 'L'histoire du Christ est un symbole, une métaphore. Mais on croyait autrefois que les métaphores se produisent comme événements dans le monde. Dieu est le suprême poète'.
9. *IP* 138: 'Le renoncement au pouvoir de penser à la première personne, c'est l'abandon de tous les biens pour suivre le Christ'.
10. *C3* 53: 'Ils étaient dans un tel état qu'ils ne pouvaient pas s'empêcher de nourrir ceux qui avaient faim, d'habiller ceux qui étaient nus; ils ne le faisaient aucunement pour le Christ, ils ne pouvaient pas s'empêcher de le faire parce que la compassion du Christ était en eux'.
11. *IP* 166: ' Quand on sait cela, on sait qu'on vit dans la médiation divine, non pas comme un poisson dans la mer, mais comme une goutte d'eau dans la mer. En nous, hors de nous, ici-bas, dans le royaume de Dieu, nulle part il n'y a autre chose. Et la médiation, c'est exactement la même chose que l'Amour'.

Towards a Conclusion

'Where does she fit in?' Thus the cry of so many when confronted with the richness and complexity of Simone Weil's thought, reacting to a very human need to be able to categorise, to show affiliation, intellectual ancestors and descendents. In all areas of life we want order, continuity, a sense of the overall coherence of the human enterprise. In the case of Simone Weil, however, any approach which seeks to identify her with any '-ism', any school, is doomed to failure. I hope to have shown some of her intellectual ancestors in the course of this study, but in the twentieth century she has affiliations with few of the major intellectual currents in France, and remains properly unclassifiable. In her lifetime she shunned the intellectual milieux of Paris, whither aspiring talent was irresistibly drawn, and preferred the relative obscurity of the provinces, and the circle of syndicalist teachers with whom she felt at home. Even when in Paris, she tended to frequent groups such as the *Nouveaux Cahiers* rather than more fashionable circles. Thus she seems sometimes to have lived in a different world from that of the pre-war capital, in spite of her tremendous involvement in the events of the time.

She was both fully in touch and profoundly out of tune with much of the first half of the twentieth century. She was fundamentally anti-individualistic: the only part of a human being that had any importance as far as she was concerned was the 'infinitely small' impersonal part that aspired and belonged elsewhere. Her total commitment to this part alienated her from movements such as Surrealism, with its emphasis on gratuity and its irresponsibility. In her political philosophy, her early writings show everywhere a critique of major currents: Marxism for its conceptual flaws; syndicalism for its short-sightedness, its disregard for truth and its impotence; and the regimes in the USSR and Germany for their totalitarianism. The spiritual theory of work and order in society which she developed towards the end of her life is no less uncompromising in its rejection of ready-made solutions, and is even more clearly hers and hers alone. The goals in fact remain the same; they simply come more sharply into focus.

Her refusal to belong to any school of thought is doubtless part of the reason that she has never given rise to one. Her vocation was strictly personal, and neither she nor her thought has ever become the object of a cult. Her refusal also to systematise, her acceptance of existence with all its contradictions, makes it difficult to talk about a 'Weilian' philosophy, although I hope to have demonstrated the overall unity of her thought. In addition, her obviously heterodox attitude to the institutions representing various bodies of thought — the Catholic Church and certain political groupings, notably on the Left — has made these bodies wary of what she was trying to say. She cannot, however, be viewed through the necessarily restricting frame of any body of dogma. If she is anything she is a Platonist, but there again of a very particular kind. In that affiliation, moreover, she is indeed a lone figure in the twentieth century.

She has always attracted and exercised a profound influence on individual figures, however. Albert Camus, who was responsible for getting much of her writing into print with Gallimard, held the view that any reconstruction of postwar France would have to take Simone Weil's ideas into account. Boris Souvarine — another writer condemned by the orthodox Left for heterodoxy — said of her that she was the only intellect the workers' movement had produced in years. T.S.Eliot was moved to write a very positive introduction to the American translation of *L'Enracinement*. In America, too, well-known writers and critics such as Dorothy Day, founder of *The Catholic Worker*, and Susan Sontag have shown great appreciation of Simone Weil's philosophy, and played an important role in its diffusion in the United States. Poets have come under her influence, most notably Czeslaw Milosz who, over the years, has given expression to the important role she has played for him, but also the Hungarian Janos Pilinsky, George Oppen in the United States and Geoffrey Hill in England. The novelist and philosopher Iris Murdoch recognises her debt to Simone Weil, while the American novelist Flannery O'Connor also admits to having been deeply influenced by her. As well-known a figure as Sartre continued to the end of his life to make occasional mention of her, and the references made by such diverse figures as Thomas Merton, Julien Green, Alberto Moravia, Jean Guitton and Mircea Eliade, are proof if any be needed that Simone Weil is still read by, and speaks to, a wide range of writers.

The variety of such recognition should not obscure the fact that, by her own definition, she was a philosopher, a 'lover of truth'. Life for her, she tells Maurice Schumann, has never had any meaning other than the search for truth. The various aspects of her vocation are in fact held together by this search for truth, just as most of the ideas she rejected with such force she regarded as representing its opposite, untruth. Truth for her was not, however, some abstract and intellectual product of speculation: it was reality itself. The experience of truth as reality was thus of crucial importance to her. As she says: 'Truth is always experimental' (*CS* 84). She is thus the most 'rooted' of thinkers, insisting that ideas to be real have to pass the test of matter. Philosophy does not consist in an accquisition of items of knowledge, but in 'a change in the soul'.[1] In the essay in which she makes this claim, she speaks of a philosophical tradition 'as old as humanity', of which Plato is probably the best representative, but which contains also the *Baghavad Gītā* and various ancient Egyptian and Chinese texts, as well as in modern times Descartes and Kant, Lagneau, Alain and Husserl. These philosophers, in spite of a difference of vocabulary, all express the same essential 'current of pure spirituality' of which she speaks elsewhere, and which, one and changeless, represents the true philosophic tradition. It is to this tradition that she would certainly see herself as belonging, if affiliations are sought, but in order to see the unity in this apparently disparate list, it is necessary to view it from her particular perspective. Its wide scope explains in large measure how readily she can refer to different historical epochs as well as different civilisations, with no sense of having to respect chronology, or discard outworn notions. If an idea belongs to this current, it will always be relevant, because timeless. Conversely, an idea not inspired in this way will be still-born, at best a commentary on its age, but will not be a vehicle of truth. In her interpretation of this Platonic tradition, Simone Weil seems to have been a precursor of a trend which is only now, some fifty years later, making itself felt: modern philosophy, and the way in which it has looked upon the ancient Greeks, has restricted itself almost entirely to problems of knowledge, of conceptual understanding, and the idea of philosophy involving a 'change in the soul' has been distinctly unfashionable, until the recent work of a critic such as Pierre Hadot began to transform modern understanding of the Ancients. Simone Weil can certainly be seen as an early voice in this transformation.[2]

Truth is a manifestation of absolute goodness, and the search for truth is attention to goodness. Simone Weil demonstrates the unity of her thought through this search for truth when she meditates on how she came to receive orders from God even in adolescence, when she professed atheism. Then, as throughout her life, she desired absolute good, and whoever believes that the desire for good is always rewarded is not an atheist (*CS* 87).

This identification of the object of philosophy with absolute goodness makes Simone Weil's thought fundamentally ethical. Her mysticism which, from this perspective, is as it were a special case of philosophy, has as its counterpart the concern to find a basis for action in the real world, and all her analyses of action are made in the light of the goodness–necessity polarity. Because of her conviction that all human beings are equal in the order of goodness, in that each and every one aspires to the good, she is profoundly and instinctively egalitarian, while retaining a sense of hierarchy which is unusual in egalitarian philosophies. Her sense of hierarchy is an extension of her sense of order, and in its own way is also egalitarian, since it depends on the concept of consent, which is identical in every human being, and the faculty which is most closely related to absolute goodness.

Simone Weil's ethical concern reveals itself not only in the structuring of society, but in her attitude to the outside world in general. To pay attention to what is other than myself is the first and most important principle of this ethic. Attention to the other is creative of reality in the same way that a painting of genius is: it reveals reality, a reality that was there all the time, but that was obscured by the existence of my autonomous being. Decreation is thus a means to the revelation of reality, through allowing the rest of creation to exist, and has as a result both epistemological and ethical implications.

Because what she has to say concerns an orientation, which remains essentially the same from age to age, her genius tends to be at its best when dealing with universal law rather than individual detail, which is no doubt why some of her programmes for reform seem unrealisable in a modern context. At the same time her grasp of absolutes, whether it be goodness, beauty or justice, made her acutely conscious of their abuse. She is thus frequently a Cassandra warning of doom, seeing further than the ordinary players in the human drama, rather than a social reformer in the strict programmatic sense. Her capacity for a global view, however, in no way prevents her from sharing in the most intimate way possible the affliction of individuals she found on her path. This was in spite of the increasing pessimism she felt about the possibility of changing social conditions, and the ever-deepening knowledge that much affliction is an unavoidable part of the human condition, a knowledge that in many simply leads to cynicism or a retreat from the world of action. There is for her if not a conflict, at least a cause for anguish in the consciousness that the whole of a person's life is governed by relationships of force, whether between that person and the universe, or that person and other human beings, and that the faculty for seeing things otherwise is infinitely small and easily destroyed. It is also only achieved at what sometimes seems to be an excessive price in human terms, namely decreation.

The role which Simone Weil accords to the individual human being remains a problem for many readers. It often seems that the individual self has only one possibility for positive action open to it, and that is to consent to its own destruction. Furthermore, by doing this it is only accepting what is reality anyway, the fact that it does not exist in any real sense. My sense of being is founded on illusion, she posits, and even if I refuse to consent to destruction, it does not make me as an individual any more real. That this is again a question of orientation and perspective, rather than a statement of fact is clear, however, if it is pushed to its logical conclusion. By consenting to decreation, I consent to the full existence of all other creatures, but they, in so far as they are orientated towards absolute goodness, do the same on behalf of all other creatures, including myself. The vision which is then produced is much more one of individuals in a genuinely 'rooted' society, based on true justice and concern for the other, rather than the disconcerting spectacle of individuals in whom everything but the desire for good has been destroyed.

She certainly felt a strong need, however, for her individual self to be de-personalised, to become nothing but the passage of grace towards the rest of humanity. This need may help to explain in part her attitude towards her Jewishness and her femininity, both aspects of herself which were less than universal, demanding specific responses and specific patterns of behaviour to which she was not prepared to conform. But her desire to suppress them, together with what she considered to be all the other 'accidental' characteristics of her as an individual, does not make decreation into some kind of self-hatred process. If indeed there remain 'problems', and this may well be the case, they cannot be resolved on this level. To do so would be to refuse value to her thought as a whole. It is impossible (in her eyes, particularly so) that a personal defect could produce a philosophy of such positive human value in terms of compassion, justice, concern for truth, and a general affirmation of the existence of the universe.

At the same time, it is important with Simone Weil above all not simply to remain in admiration before her intellect, her mastery of a huge range of subjects and of complex abstract issues, and her apparently limitless capacity for genuine compassion. Far more important, as she remarks in a letter to her family written in London only a few months before her death, is the question: 'Is she telling the truth?'

Notes

1. 'Quelques réflexions autour de la notion de valeur', quoted in Simone Pétrement, *La Vie de Simone Weil*, II, p. 319. See also R.P. Alain Birou, 'Comment et jusqu'où Simone Weil est-elle philosophe?', *Revue Thomiste*, XCIVth year, vol. LXXXVI, no. 3, July–Sept. 1986, pp. 423–44.
2. Pierre Hadot, *Exercices spirituels et philosophie antique*, 2nd rev. and aug. edn, Paris: Etudes augustiniennes, 1987.

Chronology

Date	Simone Weil	Contemporary events
1909	(3 Feb.) Birth in Paris.	
1914	Family follows Dr Weil on his various military assignments.	Outbreak of First World War.
1918		End of First World War.
1919	Family returns to Paris.	
1920		Congrès de Tours: birth of French Communist Party.
1924	Enters Lycée Victor-Duruy as pupil of Le Senne.	
1925	Pupil of Alain at Lycée Henri-IV.	
1928	Ecole Normale Supérieure. Participation in Workers' Education and syndicalist activities.	
1929	Prepares dissertation on Descartes for *Diplôme d'Etudes Supérieures*.	Wall Street Crash. Creation of Maginot Line.
1930	Beginning of headaches.	Revolt of Annamites, Yen Bay, Tongking (now North Vietnam).
1931	Passes *Agrégation*, posted as philosophy teacher to Le Puy. Makes contact	Colonial Exhibition, Bois de Vincennes.

	with syndicalists in St-Etienne. Articles for *Libres Propos*, *L'Effort*.	
1932	Visit to Germany. Writes articles on situation there. Posted as teacher to Auxerre.	Franco-Soviet non-aggression pact.
1933	Begins writing for *La Critique Sociale* (Boris Souvarine editor). Meets Trotsky. Posted to Roanne.	Hitler becomes Chancellor.
1934	'Réflexions sur les causes de la liberté et de l'oppression sociale'. (Dec.) Enters Alsthom as factory-hand.	(Feb.) General strike throughout France. (30 June) 'Night of the long knives' in Germany. Birth of Popular Front. Pact of unity, Communists/Socialists.
1935	Work in various factories. Visit to Portugal. First 'contact with Christianity that really counted'. Posted to Bourges.	Italy invades Ethiopia.
1936	Correspondence with M. Bernard on factory life. Joins Durruti's Anarcho-Syndicalist column on Republican side in Spanish Civil War.	Electoral victory of Popular Front. Léon Blum Prime Minister. Matignon Agreements. Outbreak of Spanish Civil War.
1937	Writings on colonies. At Montana (Switzerland), meets Jean Posternak.	Fall of Blum. Fascist attacks.

	Contacts with *Nouveaux Cahiers* group. Travels to Italy. Spiritual experience in Assisi. Posted to St-Quentin.	
1938	(Jan.) Sick-leave. Solesmes. Discovers English Metaphysical poets. Spiritual experiences. Writings on colonies and approach of war.	Second Popular Front Government, lasting a month. Daladier forms government without Socialists. Hitler invades and annexes Austria.
1939	Abandons pacifist stance. Sick-leave.	(Aug.) Soviet–German pact. (Sept.) Hitler invades Poland. Britain and France declare war.
1940	Articles on Hitler. Composes 'Project for front-line nurses'. Begins work on play, *Venise sauvée*. Readings in Hindu sacred texts. (June) Leaves Paris when declared 'open city'. To Marseilles, via Nevers, Vichy. '*L' Iliade* ou le poème de la force'.	Phoney War. Hitler invades Low Countries, then France. Armistice. End of Third Republic. Division of France into two zones. Creation of Vichy régime under Maréchal Pétain. (June) De Gaulle reaches London. Broadcasts appeal for resistance.
1941	Frequents *Société d'Etudes Philosophiques de Marseille* (Gaston Berger). Introduced to Fr Perrin. Works with Gustave Thibon and on neighbouring farms as	Foundation of *Cahiers de Témoignage Chrétien*. Hitler invades Russia. Siege of Leningrad. Pearl Harbor: United States and Britain declare war on Japan.

	farm-hand. Helps distribute *Cahiers de Témoignage Chrétien*. Reads St John of the Cross, the *Upanishads*, the *Tao-te-Ching*.	
1942	Letters to Fr Perrin and Joë Bousquet. Leaves Marseilles for United States, then (Nov.) for London. (Dec.) Employed by Free French (Louis Closon). Writes night and day.	Resistance leader Jean Moulin parachuted into France. Jews in Occupied Zone obliged to wear yellow star. First meeting of *Comité général d'études*, created by Jean Moulin. 'La France libre' becomes 'La France combattante'. Monseigneur Saliège in diocesan letter protests against persecution of Jews.
1943	Texts including *L'Enracinement*. (Apr.) Enters Middlesex Hospital. (Aug.) Transferred to Ashford Sanitorium, Kent. (24 Aug.) Death in Ashford.	Weekly meat-ration in France falls to 120g. Uprising in Warsaw ghetto. Foundation of *Conseil National de la Résistance*.

Select Bibliography

Bibliography for Further Reading

For an extended bibliography of Simone Weil's writings and of secondary material up to the end of 1978, the reader is referred to my *Simone Weil: A Bibliography*, London: Grant and Cutler, 1973, and Supplement 1, 1979. Other bibliographical material is to be found in:

A. Marchetti, *Simone Weil, con una Bibliografia sistematica, estratto dagli Atti della Accademia delle Scienze dell'Istituto di Bologna*, Bologna: Tipografia Compositori, 1977.

———, *Simone Weil, la critica disvelante*, Bologna: Editrice Clueb, 1983.

George Abbott White, 'Simone Weil's Bibliography: Some Reflections on Publishing and Criticism', in idem (ed.), *Simone Weil: Interpretations of a Life*, Amherst: University of Massachusetts Press, 1981.

The *Cahiers Simone Weil*, published by the *Association pour l'étude de la pensée de Simone Weil*, contain further bibliographical information, as well as a wide variety of articles and other relevant material.

Works by Simone Weil

In French:

Attente de Dieu, 2nd edn, Paris: La Colombe, 1950
Cahiers, I, Paris: Plon, new rev. and aug. edn, 1970
Cahiers, II, Paris: Plon, new rev. and aug. edn, 1972
Cahiers, III, Paris: Plon, new rev. and aug. edn, 1974
La Condition ouvrière, Paris: Gallimard, Coll. Espoir, 1951
La Connaissance surnaturelle, Paris: Gallimard, Coll. Espoir, 1950
Ecrits historiques et politiques, Paris: Gallimard, Coll. Espoir, 1960
Ecrits de Londres et dernières lettres, Paris: Gallimard, Coll. Espoir, 1957
L'Enracinement, Paris: Gallimard, 2nd edn, Coll. Espoir, 1950

Intuitions pré-chrétiennes, Paris: La Colombe, 1951

Leçons de philosophie de Simone Weil (Roanne 1933–1934), (presented by Anne Reynaud), Paris: Plon, 1959

Lettre à un religieux, Paris: Gallimard, Coll. Espoir, 1951

Oeuvres complètes, new edn, vol. I, *Premiers essais philosophiques*, Paris: Gallimard, 1988

Oppression et liberté, Paris: Gallimard, Coll. Espoir, 1955

Pensées sans ordre concernant l'amour de Dieu, Paris: Gallimard, Coll. Espoir, 1962

La Pesanteur et la grâce, Paris: Plon, Coll. L'Epi, 1947

Poèmes, suivis de 'Venise sauvée', Lettre de Paul Valéry, Paris: Gallimard, Coll. Espoir, 1968

Réflexions sur les causes de la liberté et de l'oppression sociale, Paris: Gallimard, Coll. Idées, 1980

La Source grecque, Paris: Gallimard, Coll. Espoir, 1953

Sur la science, Paris: Gallimard, Coll. Espoir, 1965

In English

(a) Complete and collected editions

First and Last Notebooks, tr. Richard Rees, London, New York and Toronto: Oxford University Press, 1970. (*La Connaissance surnaturelle* plus translations of a pre-war notebook (1933–9) excluded from the first French edn of the *Cahiers*.)

Formative Writings, 1929–1941, ed. and tr. Dorothy Tuck McFarland and Wilhelmina Van Ness, Amherst: University of Massachusetts Press, 1987. (Translations of SW's dissertation on Descartes written for the *Diplôme d'Etudes Supérieures*; texts from the *Ecrits historiques el politiques* on Germany, and on war and peace; the 'Journal d'usine' from *La Condition ouvrière*; and an essay on philosophy published in the *Cahiers du Sud*.)

Gateway to God, ed. David Raper, Glasgow: Wm Collins (Fontana Books), 1974. (Translations of SW's poem, 'La Porte', selections from the *Cahiers*, essays from *Pensées sans ordre* . . . , and the 'Lettre à un religieux'.)

Gravity and Grace (*La Pesanteur et la grâce*), tr. Emma Craufurd, London: Routledge & Kegan Paul, 1952

Intimations of Christianity (*Intuitions pré-chrétiennes*), tr. Elizabeth Chase Geissbühler, London: Routledge & Kegan Paul, 1957

Lectures on Philosophy (*Leçons de philosophie de Simone Weil*), tr. Hugh Price, introd. Peter Winch, Cambridge: Cambridge University Press, 1978

Letter to a Priest (*Lettre à un religieux*), tr. Arthur F. Wills, London: Routledge & Kegan Paul, 1953; New York: Putnam's Sons, 1954

The Need for Roots (*L'Enracinement*), tr. Arthur F. Wills, Preface by T.S. Eliot, London: Routledge & Kegan Paul, 1952; New York: Putnam's Sons, 1953

The Notebooks of Simone Weil, tr. Arthur F. Wills, 2 vols., London: Routledge & Kegan Paul; New York: Putnam's Sons, 1956. (Translation of the original edn of the *Cahiers*, Paris: Plon, 1951, 1953, 1956.)

On Science, Necessity and the Love of God, tr. Richard Rees, London, New York, Toronto: Oxford University Press, 1968. (Translations of essays from *Pensées sans ordre* . . . , *Attente de Dieu*, *Sur la science*, *La Source grecque*, *La Condition ouvrière*, and from the journal *Cahiers du Sud*.)

Oppression and Liberty (*Oppression et liberté*), tr. Arthur F. Wills and John Petrie, London: Routledge & Kegan Paul, 1958

Selected Essays (1934–43), tr. Richard Rees, London: Oxford University Press, 1962. (Translations of texts from *Ecrits historiques et politiques*, *Ecrits de Londres* . . . and *Oppression et liberté*.)

Seventy Letters, tr. Richard Rees, London: Oxford University Press, 1965. (Translations of 'Un appel aux ouvriers de R[osières]' from *La Condition ouvrière*, plus letters from *Sur la science*, *Ecrits historiques* . . . , *Pensées sans ordre* . . . , *La Condition ouvrière*, *Ecrits de Londres* . . . , *Oppression et liberté*, and a number previously unpublished.)

Simone Weil: An Anthology, ed. Siân Miles, London: Virago Books, 1986. (Collection of previously existing translations from *Seventy Letters*, *Gravity and Grace*, *Oppression and Liberty*, *Waiting on God*, plus the McCarthy translation of the *Iliad* essay, and a translation by Miles of an essay from *La Condition ouvrière*.)

The Simone Weil Reader, ed. with an introd. by George A. Panichas, New York: David McKay, 1977. (Contains very broad selection of essays from *Waiting on God*, *Oppression and Liberty*, *Selected Essays*, *On Science, Necessity and the Love of God*, and *Intimations of Christianity*; letters from *Seventy Letters* and the previously uncollected letter published in *Politics* under the title 'What is a Jew?'; extracts from *The Need for Roots, Gravity and Grace, The Notebooks of Simone Weil* and *First and Last Notebooks*; and two poems tr. William Burford, previously published in *The Phoenix*.)

Waiting on God (*Attente de Dieu*), tr. Emma Craufurd, London: Routledge and Kegan Paul, 1951

(b) Individual essays

'*The Iliad* or the Poem of Force' ('*L'Iliade* ou le poème de la force'), tr. Mary McCarthy, *Politics* (NY), II, 11, Nov. 45, pp. 321–31. (Also repr. in *Simone Weil: An Anthology*, ed. Miles, pp. 182–215.)

'Reflections on War' ('Réflexions sur la guerre'), tr. unspecified, *Politics* (NY), II, 2, Feb. 45, pp. 51–5

'Words and War' ('Ne recommençons pas la guerre de Troie'), tr. Bowden Broadwater, *Politics* (NY), III, 3, Mar. 46, pp. 69–73

Biography

Cabaud, Jacques, *Simone Weil: A Fellowship in Love*, London: Harvill, 1964; New York: Channel Press, 1965

Pétrement, Simone, *Simone Weil: A Life* (tr. by Raymond Rosenthal of *La Vie de Simone Weil*, Paris: Fayard, 1973), New York: Pantheon Books, 1977

Critical Studies on Simone Weil

Anderson, David, *Simone Weil*, London: S.C.M. Press, 1971

Canciani, Domenico, Gabriella Fiori, Giancarlo Gaeta, Adriano Marchetti, *Simone Weil: la passione della verità*, Brescia: Editrice Morcelliana, 1984

Davy, Marie-Magdeleine, *The Mysticism of Simone Weil* (tr. by Cynthia Rowland of *Introduction au message de Simone Weil*, Paris: Plon, 1954), London: Rockliff; Boston: Beacon Press, 1951

Kahn, Gilbert (ed.), *Simone Weil, philosophe, historienne et mystique*, Paris: Aubier Montaigne, 1978

Narcy, Michel, *Simone Weil: Malheur et beauté du monde*, Paris: Edns du Centurion, 1967

Perrin, Joseph-Marie, O.P., and Gustave Thibon, *Simone Weil as We Knew Her* (tr. by Emma Craufurd of *Simone Weil telle que nous l'avons connue*, Paris: La Colombe, 1952), London: Routledge & Kegan Paul, 1953

Perrin, Joseph-Marie, O.P., *Mon Dialogue avec Simone Weil*, Preface by André A. Devaux, Paris: Nouvelle Cité, 1984

Rees, *Simone Weil: A Sketch for a Portrait*, London: Oxford University Press, 1966; Carbondale: S. Illinois Univ. Press, 1966

Schlette, Heinz Robert and André A. Devaux (eds.), *Simone Weil: Philosophie, Religion*, Frankfurt on Main: Verlag Josef Knecht, 1985

Schumann, Maurice, *La Mort née de leur propre vie (Péguy, Simone Weil, Gandhi)*, Paris: Fayard, 1974

Springsted, Eric O., *Simone Weil and the Suffering of Love*, Preface by Robert Coles, Cambridge, MA: Cowley Publications, 1986

Vetö, Miklos, *La Métaphysique religieuse de Simone Weil*, Paris: Vrin, 1971

White, George Abbott (ed.), *Simone Weil: Interpretations of a Life*, Amherst: University of Massachusetts Press, 1981

Index

Abel, 143
Alain (pseud. of Emile Chartier), 9, 10, 12, 13, 14, 18, 23, 105, 153
Algeciras, Act of, 81
Algeria, 39, 46
Alsthom (Société), 27, 33
America, 42, 44, 152
Annamites, 14
Anschluss, 34
Apocalypse, 77
Antigone (Sophocles), 29
Aquinas, Saint Thomas, 75, 83
Arjuna, 64
Armistice (25 June 1940), 38
Ashford (England), 44, 45
Assisi, 33
D'Aubigné, Agrippa, 93
Austria, 34, 92
Auxerre, 19, 20, 21

Bach, Johann Sebastian, 111
Balzac, Honoré de, 18
Belgium, 38
Belleville (M and Mme), 29, 30
Bergery, Gaston, 34
Berlin, 20
Bernanos, Georges,
 Les Grands Cimetières sous la lune, 32
Bernard (engineer, Rosières), 29
Bhagavad Gītā, 64, 153
Birou, R.P. Alain, 156
Blum, Léon, 31, 33, 34
La Boétie, Étienne de, 93
Bouglé, C., 13
Bourges, 28, 29, 30, 34
Bousquet, Joë, 36, 46
Brunschvicg, Henri, 13, 15
Buber, Martin, 83
Buddhism, Buddhist, 76

Cabaud, Jacques, 3, 13
Cahiers du Sud, 40, 99
Cahiers de Témoignage Chrétien, 40
Camus, Albert, 152
Carcopino (Minister of Education), 39
Carthage, Carthaginian, 78
Casablanca, 42
Cathars, Catharism, 40, 99, 100
C G T (*Confédération Générale du travail*), 16, 18
C G T U (*Confédération Générale du Travail Unitaire*), 18, 22
Chamberlain, Neville, 36
Christ 35, 41, 48, 56, 67, 76, 79, 115, 125, 128, 140, 141, 142, 143, 144, 145, 146, 147, 148, 150
Church, Roman Catholic 40, 41, 44, 67, 73, 74, 75, 76, 77, 83, 99, 100, 128, 152
Closon, Louis, 43, 45
Communism, 10, 16, 17, 18, 20, 21, 61
Communist Party (French), 10, 21, 22
'Conseil National de la Résistance', 44
Constantine (Algeria), 39
Constantine, Emperor, 77
Copeau, Edi, 14
Copeau, Jacques, 14
Corneille, Pierre, 80
Couturier, Fr, 43
Crete, 142
Crusades, 73, 100
Czechoslovakia, 34, 36, 37

Daniel, 143
Darwin, Darwinism, 95
David, Marie-Louise, 40
Day, Dorothy, 152
Declaration of the Rights of Man (1789), 44, 85, 97
Declaration of Independence (American), 85
de Gaulle, General, 38, 39, 96, 97
Demeter, 138
Descartes, René, 15, 93, 153
Detœuf, Auguste, 27, 33, 34, 111, 112
Dionysos, 142
Druids, 78
Durruti, 31

Ecole Normale Supérieure (rue d'Ulm) 12, 13, 14, 15, 24
L'Effort (Lyon) 19
Egypt, Egyptian (Ancient), 87, 103, 142
Einsiedeln, 35
Eliade, Mircea, 152
Eliot, T.S., 152
Enlightenment, 72
Enoch, 143

167

Etoile nord-africaine, 34

Fascism, 30, 32, 80
First World War, 7, 31
Florence, 32
Francis of Assisi, Saint, 33, 48
Free French Forces, 42, 43, 44, 45, 53, 85, 102

Genesis, 55, 71, 116
Germany, 2, 8, 20, 21, 22, 23, 30, 32, 33, 34, 36, 38, 61, 72, 78, 80, 81, 92, 151
Gide, André, 89
Giraudoux, Jean, 37
Gospel, Saint John's, 147
Greece, Greeks (Ancient), 60, 61, 70, 73, 74, 78, 85, 94, 105, 126, 138, 142, 144, 147, 150, 153
Green, Julien, 152
Groupe d'éducation sociale (rue Falguière), 11, 13
Guitton, Jean, 152

Hades, 138
Hadot, Pierre, 154, 156
Harlem, 43
Hebrews, Ancient, 71, 83
Hegel, Georg Wilhelm Friedrich, 68, 69
Herbert, George, 'Love', 35, 144
Herder, Johann Gottfried, 91
Hill, Geoffrey, 152
Hitler, Adolf, 2, 20, 23, 34, 36, 37, 38, 60, 61, 78, 79, 80, 81
Holland, 38
Honnorat, Hélène, 42
L'Humanité, 17
Husserl, Edmund, 153

Iliad, The, 40, 60, 63, 68, 73
Inquisistion, 73
Israel (Ancient), 70, 71, 77
Italy, 30, 32, 34

Jaffier, 101, 144
Jehovah, 70
Joan of Arc, 60, 80
Job, 143
John of the Cross, Saint, 130, 131
Joseph, 71
Judaism, 40, 67, 69, 70, 71, 72, 73, 75

Kant, Emmanuel, 18, 153
Krishna, 65

Lagneau, 153
Lamartine, Alphonse Marie-Louis-de, 93

Languedoc civilisation (12th Century), 99, 100, 101
Leahy, Admiral, 42
Le Puy-en-Velay, 15, 16, 17, 18, 19, 21, 23, 33
Levinas, Emmanuel, 83
Libres Propos, 13
Lille, 32
Liverpool, 43
logos, 142, 147
London, 38, 42, 43, 72, 84, 85, 88, 96, 124, 125, 156
Louis XIV, 79, 80
De Lussy, Florence, 83
Luxemburg, Rosa, 22
Lycée Henri-IV, 9, 10, 12, 13, 43
Lycée Montaigne, 8
Lycée Victor Duruy, 14

Machiavelli, Niccolò, 62
Mallarmé, Stéphane, 93
Maritain, Jacques, 42
Marseilles, 38, 39, 40, 42, 60, 72, 99, 115, 146
Martinet, Marcel, 18
Marx, Karl, 1, 19, 22, 62, 68, 69, 82, 110
Marxism, Marxist, 14, 106, 151
Maurin, 31
Mazargues (Marseilles), 39, 40
Merton, Thomas, 152
Messali Hadj, 34
Milosz, Czeslaw, 152
Mithra, Mithraism, 77
Molière, 93
Monatte, Pierre, 18
Montaigne, Michel de, 93
Montana (Switzerland), 32
Montesquieu, Charles Louis de Secondat, Baron de, 93
Moravia, Alberto, 152
Morocco, 39, 42, 81, 83
Moses, 70, 83
Mozart, Wolfgang Amadeus, 32
Munich Agreement, 36
Murdoch, Iris, 152

Napoleon I, 79, 128
Naurois, Abbé de, 44
Nazi, Nazis, 2, 20, 34, 72, 78
Nerval, Gérard de, 93
Nevers, 38, 41
New York, 38, 42, 43, 125
Nice, 36
Nimrod, 143
Noah, 143
Nouveaux Cahiers, Les, 33, 34, 151

O'Connor, Flannery, 152

Old Testament, 73
Oppen, George, 152
Osiris, 142

Paris, 7, 22, 23, 24, 31, 36, 80, 114, 151
Pascal, Blaise, 7
Perrin, Fr Joseph-Marie, 8, 24, 28, 33, 35, 40, 41, 47, 115, 122
Persephone, 138
Pétain, Maréchal, 38, 96
Pétrement, Simone, 3, 47, 49, 156
Philip, André, 43, 45
Pilinsky, János, 152
Plato, Platonism, 18, 54, 55, 56, 61, 62, 68, 74, 137, 141, 143, 144, 147, 152, 153
The Republic, 74, 143
Popular Front, 29, 33, 92
Portugal, 28, 39, 120
Posternak, Jean, 32, 33
P O U M (*Partido obrero de unificación marxista*), 31
Povoa do Varzini (Portugal), 47
Prometheus, 142, 143
Pythagoras, Pythagoreans, 141, 142, 146

Rabelais, François, 93
Racine, Jean, *Phèdre*, 93
Rees, Sir Richard, 48, 65
Renan, Auguste, 103
Retz, Cardinal de, 93
Reville, 15
Revolution, French, 85
Révolution Prolétarienne, La, 22
Reynaud, Anne, 23
Rheims, 22
Rhodes, Cecil, 80
Richelieu, 79, 80
Roanne, 21, 22, 23, 105
Rome, Roman, 33, 37, 59, 77, 78, 80, 81, 83, 85, 101, 104
Rosières, 29
Rossini, 32
Roubaud, Louis, 14
Rousseau, Jean-Jacques, 93, 99
Russia, 22, 23, 80, 151

St-Etienne, 18, 19, 23
St-Quentin, 17, 33
Saint-Réal, Abbé de, 100
Santa Maria degli Angeli (Church of), 48
Sartre, Jean-Paul, 152
Scève, Maurice, 93
Schumann, Maurice, 43, 45, 121, 122, 123, 153
Second World War, 2, 20, 25, 31, 61

Shem, 143
Solesmes, 35
Sontag, Susan, 152
Sorbonne, 12, 15, 78
Souvarine, Boris, 10, 21, 22, 27, 152
Spanish Civil War, 2, 25, 26, 27, 128
Spanish Empire, 100
Stoicism, Stoic, 137
Sudeten, 34
Surrealism, 151

Tacitus, 78
Tailleferre, Germaine, 8
Tao-te-Ching, Taoist, 130
Théophile de Viau, 93
Thévenon, Urbain and Albertine, 18, 19
Thibon, Gustave, 41, 42
Tolstoy, Leo, 18
Toulouse, 38, 99, 100, 103
Trotsky, Leon, 23
Troy, Trojan, 73

United States of America, *see* America
Upanishads, 40
U S S R, *see* Russia

Venice, 100, 101, 104, 144
Verdi, 32
Vernon, John, 35
Vichy, 38, 39, 40, 41, 43
Vietnam, 14
Vigny, Alfred de, 93
Villon, François, 93
Virgil, 79

Weil, André, 7, 8, 37, 42, 43, 48
Weil, Dr Bernard, 7, 20, 28
Weil, Mme Selma, 7, 8, 16, 20, 28, 29
Weil, Simone, *passim*
  'Antigone', 29
  'Un appel aux ouvriers de R[osières]', 29
  Attente de Dieu, 47, 48, 55, 56, 60, 74, 76, 83, 133, 134
  'Autobiographie spirituelle', 47
  Cahiers, Vol. I, 57, 59, 64, 66, 118, 119, 129, 132
  Cahiers, Vol. II, 56, 57, 58, 64, 66, 75, 82, 104, 123, 126, 127, 128, 140, 143, 144, 146, 148, 150
  Cahiers, Vol. III, 66, 69, 71, 76, 77, 82, 109, 131, 134, 144, 150
  'Le Christianisme et la vie des champs', 115
  La Condition ouvrière, 27, 107, 108, 111, 112, 113, 117, 119, 139, 141,

142, 150
La Connaissance surnaturelle, 56, 66, 68, 77, 82, 83, 105, 119, 122, 124, 125, 126, 133, 144, 150, 153, 154
Ecrits historiques et politiques, 66, 78, 79, 81
Ecrits de Londres et dernières lettres, 44, 48, 65, 66, 72, 84, 85, 88, 96, 97, 98, 99, 102, 103, 111, 118, 122, 133, 134
L'Enracinement, 47, 66, 78, 80, 81, 83, 84, 85, 86, 87, 89, 90, 91, 92, 94, 95, 96, 102, 103, 105, 110, 116, 117, 118, 119, 152
'Etude pour une déclaration des obligations envers l'être humain', 86
'Expérience de la vie d'usine', 113
Formative Writings, 47
'L'Iliade, ou le poème de la force', 36, 40, 60, 109
Intimations of Christianity, 48
Intuitions pré-chrétiennes, 55, 58, 59, 134, 136, 140, 145, 146, 147, 149
'Journal d'usine', 27
Leçons de philosophie de Simone Weil (Anne Reynaud), 47, 105
Lettre à un religieux, 43, 76
'Luttons-nous pour la justice?', 88
'Le Maroc, ou la prescription en matière de vol', 81
'Ne recommençons pas la guerre de Troie', 61
Oppression and Liberty, 47

Oppression et liberté, 49, 63, 66, 68, 69, 82, 83, 105, 107, 109
Pensées sans ordre concernant l'amour de Dieu, 49, 55, 82, 83, 103, 115, 119, 146, 150
La Pesanteur et la grâce, 130
'Un peu d'histoire à propos du Maroc', 81
Poèmes, suivis de 'Venise sauvée', 104, 150
'Profession de foi', 53, 54
'Prologue' (*La Connaissance surnaturelle*), 144
'Quelques réflexions sur les origines de l'hitlérisme', 78
'Réflexions sur les causes de la liberté et de l'oppression sociale', 24, 46, 63, 105, 107
'Réflexions sur la révolte', 44
Selected Essays, 48, 65
Seventy Letters, 48
Simone Weil: An Anthology, 48
La Source grecque, 59, 60, 62, 66, 83
'Du temps', 107
'Le travail physique consenti . . .', 116
Venise sauvée, 40, 100, 144
Waiting on God, 47
Weil, Sylvie, 43

Yen Bay, 47

Zagreus, 142
Zeus, 73